The Wisdener Manual

by Bill Furmedge

The Collectors' Club Guide to the Yellow Bible

Introduction

When I sat down to write this introduction two pieces of information had reached me which made me realise once again that we are all temporary owners of our beloved *Wisdens* and whether we buy for the pleasure of reading or the thrill of collecting it all comes down to the fact that there is someone, who will never be known to us, who will one day pick up the 1965 we now treasure and say something like, 'it has been looked after.'

In early 2013 I received a telephone call asking if I could possibly send a recent copy of The Wisdener as a friend of the caller had mentioned it. The Wisden Collectors' Club (WCC) had been growing in membership steadily since its launch in mid-2011, but this was the first referral I had ever received, so I gladly asked the caller for his name and address with the promise that the latest edition of the club newsletter would be posted straight away.

"David Rayvern Allen" came the reply.

Those of you who have had the misfortune to be stuck on the telephone with me while I wax lyrical about *Wisden*, my family, my beloved and always frustrating Lancashire or my equally beloved and permanently frustrating Liverpool FC will know that I am both amazed and flattered that cricket writers whom I have admired and read for decades have shown an interest in The Wisdener, and indeed many have contributed articles or even become WCC members. So, when the caller gave me his name I was, once again, flattered to say the least. The newsletter was duly sent out and I received a call around a week later thanking me. He also said after a nice chat, "Keep up the good work".

David was added to our membership and over the course of the following eighteen months I was fortunate enough to meet him at various auctions and at the 2014 *Wisden* launch dinner. He gave me so much positive and kind encouragement and feedback on The Wisdener and on my first little publishing venture, *What Wisden Means To Me*. He even contributed a lovely article for The Wisdener, which has been included in this publication.

Back to the first line of my introduction: The first piece of information I received was that David had passed away in early October 2014 after a long battle with cancer and my first thought was not one of sadness because he had died, but sadness because I wouldn't be able to talk to him at auctions, and sadness because he wouldn't call me after he received the latest newsletter; then I re-read an email exchange we had when he was submitting his article for The Wisdener. From a man who had written 43 books, been a Producer at The BBC, an archivist for Lord's and written the acclaimed biography of John Arlott, amongst many other things; he wrote at the end of an email in

1

reference to his article, "Is it ok?" Whether through politeness or simple courtesy the fact that a wonderful cricket writer was making sure his article was good enough absolutely stunned me. I replied very quickly, "It is excellent, thank you".

What I do is quite straight-forward: put simply, I sell *Wisdens,* but along the way I get to meet some wonderful people and I am sad that I could not have spent more time knowing David Rayvern Allen.

The second piece of information that came to me was from a man who had called me to let me know that his *Wisden* 1930 had arrived. His initial call had been to try and trace the *Wisden* that his grandfather had appeared in, not for himself, but for his 10-year-old grandson. Initially he had said that G.D. Durtnall had played for Kent 2nd XI in one of the years after WW1.

I had checked every *Wisden* up to 1925 to no avail, but after telling him that I could not find any record I decided to look through the rest of the 1920s, no joy; last resort, the 1930s and on page 566 of the 1930, there he is. Scoring 60 and 3 in the single match that he had played in.

The current Mr. Durtnall was overjoyed. He rang to confirm safe receipt of the 1930 and he added a footnote. Telling me that he had initially been given my name, and number by David Rayvern Allen.

The world is full of coincidences, chance meetings and encounters, and cricket has this habit of bringing people from all different walks of life together; in fact, *Wisden* has the habit of doing it more. For collectors of *Wisden* are a unique and engaging band, we value the traditions and achievements of the past whilst fearing and in the same moment being excited by the cricket that lies ahead. We admire and relish the feats, the players, the Tests, the county games of years long gone and we frown and we curse and we smile at the achievements, the players, the Tests, and the county games of now. We are mere custodians of our beloved *Wisdens* and long may we enjoy them.

The structure of the Manual is quite straight-forward. The first part concentrates on *Wisden* and collecting, interspersed with selective extracts from The Wisdener, the newsletter of the Wisden Collectors' Club. Thereafter I have taken articles and further extracts from the newsletter which I hope readers will find of interest. I want readers to be able to dip in and out of the Manual and that is why I have structured it as I have.

There are a number of people who have helped with the putting together of this Manual and a big thank you is owed to Andrew Renshaw, who despite having enough on his plate helped a great deal with the proofing. I apologise now for any errors and there will be some, these are down to me. If I have omitted to type *Wisden* in italics on every occasion then I expect to be severely reprimanded.

The danger in listing people to thank is that I will omit people who have contributed so again, If I have missed anyone out, my apologies:

Peter Ackermann, Lawrence Booth, Glynn Burgess, Steve Calcott, Prof. John Chartres, Steve Coleman, Steve Crispin, Nick Davies, Ian Derbyshire, Fraser Dillingham, Giles Falconer, Noor Farid, John Farr, Peter Foster, David Frith, Lorraine Furmedge, Edward Grant, Brian Hagan, Martin Haggett, Tom Healy, Nigel Heath, Murray Hedgcock, David Jenkins, John Jewiss, Mark Jones, David Kelly, Paul Kilmartin, Norman Kinney, Mark Lawley, Richard Lawrence, Mark Leader, Nick Loot, Peter Mortensen, Steve Pickard, David Pickering, John Pratt, David Rayvern Allen, Andrew Renshaw, Jonathan Rice, Stephen Slater, Terry Smith, John Sumner, John Swain, Michael Waby, David Wild.

I hope you enjoy this guide to *Wisden*. In fact, if you enjoy it just half as much as I have enjoyed putting it together, I will be delighted.

Bill Furmedge
November 2014

Contents

Wisden

An insight into the history of Wisden
Since the first Wisden was published in 1864 there have been two main formats. Initially there was just a paperback edition, but in 1896 Wisden complemented the paperback with a hard cloth version. The following is a guide to the various formats that have evolved over Wisden's history and some of the interesting anomalies along the way

Other books have been published over the years incorporating the *Wisden* name – *Wisden* anthologies, *Wisden* on Test Cricket, the excellent *Wisden on The Great War* and many more. This guide deals only with the yearly cricket almanack, although some publication dates are listed below. A further look at the different formats of the almanack can be found elsewhere.

As an introduction, the following is a chronological breakdown:
1864 The first *Wisden* published, in paperback. The covers were pale pink, and this colour was used until the 1872 edition.
1872 Until 1877, the colour of the covers was pink/buff.
1889 The first photographic plate appeared.
1896 The hard cloth edition was published.
1896 A single photo plate of W. G. Grace appeared.
1923-1924 John *Wisden's* Rugby Football Almanack was published. Only a further two editions, 1924-25 and 1925-1926, were issued.
1938 The paper covers were replaced by a linen cloth material, the thicker covers giving the pages better protection.
1944 *An Index to Wisden*, 1864-1943, compiled by Rex Pogson, was published.
1960 The publishers of *Wisden*, Sporting Handbooks, commissioned Billings and Son to reprint in paperback format the first fifteen editions (1864-78 inclusive). These were sold as a boxed set for £40. Individual editions were available at £3 3s (£3.15). It is believed that 150 copies of each year were produced, with 100 sold as sets. A further set was published by a different company, Lowe & Brydone, in 1974. This set sold for £50, with 100 on offer, and a further 50 copies of each year were also available.
1965 A yellow 'Dust Wrapper', also referred to as a 'Dust Jacket' or a 'sleeve', was introduced on the hard cloth or hardback edition, once again giving protection and allowing the publishers to highlight each almanack's content on the front cover.
1979 The first *Wisden Anthology 1864-1900* edited by Benny Green was published.
1980 The second *Wisden Anthology 1900-1940* edited by Benny Green was published.

1982 The third *Wisden* Anthology 1940-1963 edited by Benny Green was published.

1983 *Wisden* granted a license to the Willows Publishing Company to reprint each almanack from 1879.

1983 The fourth *Wisden Anthology 1963-1982* edited by Benny Green was published.

1985 *An Index To Wisden, 1864-1984* compiled by Derek Barnard was published.

1988 *The Illustrated Wisden Anthology 1864-1988* edited by Benny Green was published.

1991 *Wisden* reproduced the first fifteen editions as a box set; differing from the earlier reprints as each edition had brown boards and the full set was sold in a yellow presentation case.

1995 *Wisden* published 100 Leather-Bound editions signed by the editor.

1996 *Wisden* increased the number of Leather-Bound editions to 150.

1998 The first issue of *Wisden Cricketers Almanack Australia* was published by Hardie Grant Books. 'Ozden', as it was called, ran for eight editions.

2003 Since 1938 the front cover of the *Wisden* Linen Cloth edition and from 1965 the dust jacket had depicted two Victorian gentlemen and a main list of contents, but in 2003 the image and the contents were replaced by a photograph. The first front cover photograph was of Michael Vaughan.

2004 Aimed exclusively at the home market, *Wisden* India was published, which ran until 2009.

2006 A Large Format edition was introduced, housed in a slip case.

2013 The first edition of *Wisden* India Almanack under agreement between Fidelis World FZ LLC and John Wisden & Co was published.

2014 *Wisden on The Great War* edited by Andrew Renshaw was published.

Wisden anomalies and quirks

It is not possible to include every nuance of Wisden, every missing letter or changing front cover style, and it would be impractical to try. Many Wisden collectors will have spotted their own anomaly in a certain edition or speculated on why a certain year is rarer than a later year. It is not just the content that stimulates debate, but the Wisden itself.

1864 The first edition had a list of the Derby winners from 1780, along with the length and years of opening for a large number of canals. It also included a monthly calendar of important cricketing as well as historical dates. This calendar, which included information such as the Duke of Wellington's birthday (September 14), was included up to 1878, and in 1879 just a standard calendar appeared. The calendar was then included in every edition to 1941. The 1864 almanack cost one shilling.

1864 It is titled The Cricketer's Almanack.

1865 The second edition describes the legalising of over-arm bowling.

1867 *Wisden* included "The births and deaths of celebrated cricketers" and the first advertisement appeared, for John *Wisden* and Co's patent Catapulta.

1868 The calendar pages for April, May & August in this edition are for 1867.

1869 This edition contains the first record of an overseas tour to England, undertaken by a team of Australian Aboriginals.

1870 This almanack was the first to include bowling analyses and match descriptions.

1870 The **1870** became John Wisden's Cricketer's Almanack

1874 & 1875 It is believed that these editions were the first to be completely sold out upon publication. It is thought that the 1875 edition was actually printed in late 1874. There are three different 1875 editions. The pagination of each is different: 212, 214 and 214 with an additional blank page at the rear (totalling 216 pages). To this day the 1875 is arguably the rarest of all. It is generally believed that this edition had the least number printed. There is also a school of thought that suggests a fire at the Mortlake factory where *Wisden* was printed destroyed most of the 1875 run. The 'fire' theme crops up later in *Wisdens'* history, during WW2.

1875 Page 238, 'Umpires and where to find them': 25 umpires are listed, two at the same address, and five gave their addresses as Inns.

1876 Closer examination of an original 1876 will find that string was used alongside the spine to help bind the pages together.

1878 & 1879 For both these editions a different quality of paper was used for the front and back covers. This gave the colours a shiny look and over time the lettering has had a tendency to fade.

1878 The back cover of the *Wisden* carries an advertisement for a book published by *Wisden* entitled *Oxford v Cambridge*. When *Wisden* reproduced the 1864-78 box set in 1991, the wrong back page was used.

1880s For most editions in this decade, and many for previous years, the binding behind the spine paper is approximately one centimetre from the top and the bottom of the book; this causes erosion of the spine paper at the string position, and it is very common to find paperbacks from the pre-1890 years that have spine paper missing from the top and the bottom.

1883 This *Wisden* contained the first advertisement to appear at the front of the almanack. It followed the internal title page, and was for Thurston's billiard tables.

1887 This was the first *Wisden* to have lettering on the spine.

1887 & 1888 The quality of the paper used for these editions was different to that used for the other 1880s and the covers and spine have a tendency to darken over time.

1889 The editor, Charles F. Pardon, decided to honour six of the game's most successful bowlers of the previous season and this celebration was a major factor in the almanack selling out and a second print being published. The six were:

> Charles Thomas Bryan Turner (Australia)
> John James Ferris (Australia)
> Samuel Moses James Woods (Australia)
> George Alfred Lohmann (Surrey and England)
> Robert Peel (Yorkshire and England)
> John Briggs (Nottinghamshire and England)

1889 This edition was also the first to contain a photo plate. This contained images of the 'Six Great Bowlers' (named above). The plate was protected by a thin sheet of tissue paper. Owing to the chemicals used in the production of the plate, both the tissue paper and the plate tend to have a lot of foxing.

1889 to 1901 Each edition had two print runs.

1896 W.G. Grace was the sole cricketer mentioned in the role of honour in the almanack of 1896. It is interesting to note that in the entire history of *Wisden*, on only four occasions has a single player received the accolade of being the single cricketer of the year:

> 1896 W.G.Grace
> 1913 John Wisden
> 1921 P.F. Warner
> 1926 J.B. Hobbs

A photograph of each of the four players appeared in their respective edition.

1897 The editor, Sidney Pardon, altered the previous notes highlighting "celebrated cricketers" into the 'Five Cricketers of the Season'. This feature, changed the following year to 'Five Cricketers of the Year', has remained to this day and invariably causes much debate and speculation. A rule of the feature is that no cricketer can be given the accolade of cricketer of the year more than once.

The first Five Cricketers of the Season were:

Sidney E. Gregory (Australia)
Kumar Shri Ranjitsinhji (Sussex and England)
Thomas Richardson (Surrey and England)
Arthur Augustus Lilley (Warwickshire and England)
H. Trumble (Australia)

1897 It is believed that there was a reprint of the Hardback edition.

1898 The paperback edition was reprinted and the two editions produced an interesting anomaly. In one, the Five Cricketers of the Year photograph featured two cricketers at the top, one in the middle and two at the bottom; in the reprint for the same year, one cricketer was featured at the top, then two and two. In the same edition one has the name (correctly) P.F. Warner on the contents page, and the other has W.P. Warner.

1901 It is believed that some paperback editions were printed with the wrong year on the spine and a strip was pasted on giving the correct year.

1901 Sydney Pardon began 'Notes by the Editor'.

1903 Hinge strengtheners below the yellow paste-down pages on the inside front and back of hardback editions can be seen on pre-WW2 hardbacks. This is lacking on the 1903. Unfortunately this edition is prone to hinge cracking/creasing as a consequence.

1904 Once again, the hinge strengtheners are absent.

1904 & 1905 These two almanacks are unique in the absence of the 'k' in the word almanack on the spine. Interesting that this should occur once, but it was repeated the following year. This spelling only appears on the paperback editions.

1913 The 50th edition contained a special tribute John Wisden. The Jubilee Number, as it was referred to on the front cover, contained a print of John Wisden and some 'special recollections' of him.

1915 The use of photographs of the leading cricketers was ended, along with the need for the tissue paper. Prints were used when the page was reintroduced in 1918.

1915 There has always been speculation that *Wisden* gave away complimentary copies of the almanack each year and it is perceived that this edition was the first to include a complimentary list.

1916 Arguably the most emotive of all editions. The 1916 is generally regarded as W.G. Grace's edition as it contains a 33-page tribute to the great man. What is sometimes overlooked is that two players who had also adorned the cricketing world were also remembered, A.E. Stoddart and Victor Trumper. *Wisden* totalled 300 pages, with the obituary of WG followed by those for Stoddart and Trumper taking up 69 pages. Then there are 82 pages listing the many cricketers whose lives were lost in the first full year of WW1. Reading the 1916 edition not only leaves the reader in awe at the three wonderful careers of Grace, Stoddart and Trumper, but also deeply moved by the page upon page of obituaries that follow. Both the 1916 and 1917 editions carry no Cricketers of the Year. In 1918, 'Five School Bowlers of the Year' were praised, followed in 1919 by 'Five Public School Cricketers of the Year'.

1916 Little or no gold plating was used on the wording on the front cover and spine of the hardback edition. The misconception is that no copies have gold plating: this is deemed to be incorrect.

1919 Probably owing to post-war shortages, the 1919 edition is a little unusual. The paste-down pages on the inside front and back tend to darken and from page 163 the book has a two-toned look. The conclusion is that two different types of paper may have been used during the printing process. This occurred again in 1945, 1948 and to a lesser extent 1947.

1920s *Wisden* thrived in this decade as the game grew and other facets of the business proved extremely successful, including overseas sales of equipment, Australia being a major buyer. The pagination of *Wisden* also grew from under 500 pages at the start of the decade to nearly 700 towards the end.

1922 The front and back covers of the paperback editions were printed on to white card, as opposed to the yellow card used both prior and following. Over time the covers have a brownish shade to them. On some hardback editions the inside paste-down pages tend to fade to a whitish colour at the edges. The use of paler yellow dye is probably the reason.

1924 *Wisden* exceeded 1,000 pages for the first time.

1920's Each edition from 1927 through to 1937 included an examiner's authentication slip. Each was proof read, and rather than give the proof reader's name, a number was attributed to each one, thereby protecting the anonymity of those tasked to ensure the correctness of each edition. Understandably, errors still occurred and some editions carried an errata slip for the previous year.

1928 to 1930 The height of the Great Depression impacted on *Wisden*. The quality of the materials used on both the paperback and hardback editions was compromised. This has manifested itself in the condition of the vast majority of *Wisdens* for this period. The hardbacks tend to have creased or cracked spines, the weight of the contents causing warping and bowing. The paperbacks tend to have creased and broken spines.

1930s At various times throughout the 1930s, *Wisden* put a paper band around the paperback edition. It is not known whether or not every edition had this, but 1936, 1938 and 1939 are known for certain to have had one. The 1938 had a red band, and the 1939 green.

1932 Gold gilt was used for the last time on the hardback editions. From 1933-1936 *Wisden* changed to copper. This has resulted in some fading to the front cover lettering, but mainly to the spine.

1933 to 1939 Despite the success of the 1934 edition, a number of measures were introduced to halt the general slide in sales. In 1933 a bookmark in the shape of a cricket bat, made of card, was affixed by string to the spine, and this was produced in each paperback throughout the years 1933-1939. It is unusual to find a complete bat bookmark as the top of it, designed in the style of a true cricket bat handle, tended to bend or snap off quite easily.

1934 Sales of *Wisden* declined in the 1930s with the exception of this edition. The reason for the 1934 being popular, despite the world continuing to be in the grip of recession, was the report and analysis of the 1932-33 MCC tour of Australasia, to give it its commonly used name, the 'Bodyline series'. The 1934 edition remains a 'must have' for any collector.

1938 A new publisher was brought in to try and stem the tide of falling sales, J Whitaker & Sons Ltd. The new publishers quickly made some striking changes:

A complete index was introduced for the first time.

The counties were listed alphabetically and not in the order in which they finished the previous season's championship.

More illustrations were included.

The Laws of Cricket, featured in every edition, were moved to immediately before the details of matches played.

The 1938 hardback also changed in appearance: the year, title and edition number appeared horizontally on the spine (pictured, right), as opposed to all editions from 1896 when it had been vertical.

The front cover also changed. The editor's name, title, publication year and publishers' details were no longer all included, in place the title and year only. The 1938 Hardback also has blank pages at the front and rear, replacing the yellow paste-downs.

1938 The paperback edition also had the following changes. Prior to 1938, the paper used for the front and back covers was only marginally thicker than the paper within, so creasing and fading were commonplace. The spines particularly suffered, as frequent opening caused cracking. Therefore in 1938

Wisden (pictured below, left) introduced cloth covers to replace the paper covers. These covers were and still are yellow and not prone to fading and are referred to as 'soft back' or 'linen cloth' editions.

1941 The edition number was added at the bottom of the front cover of the hardback and this has remained the same since. From 1965 this information is on the front board below the yellow dust wrapper.

1939-1945 *Wisden* kept on printing throughout WW2; indeed, the 1940 edition contains the full details of the 1939 season, with an interesting report on Page 460:

September 1st: Manchester, Lancashire v Sussex, match drawn, "no play on third day, owing to impending war"

The War Years were naturally leaner issues, with no competitive cricket played and a reduced number of copies available to buy, hence these editions are more expensive. The linen cloth editions also have a tendency to brown, with the spines and the covers noticeably affected.

Wartime restrictions on paper meant that the print run was cut.

1941 It is thought that the print run of soft backs and hardbacks was reduced from 8,000 to 3,200, with only 800 hardbacks. It is believed that the 'complimentary' copies are not included in these numbers.

The number of pages was also reduced from 871 in 1940 to 426.

Coverage concentrated on representative matches. The Public Schools report was missing: a copy had been posted but was destroyed en route by the Luftwaffe, while the original script perished in a simultaneous air raid. Production was delayed when the publisher's offices were destroyed by enemy action at the end of 1940. This has been cited as a reason for no official records about *Wisden* being available pre-1940. But this does beg the question, was there only one set of accounts? It could be argued that since the nineteenth century, companies had to have two, and in some cases three, sets of company records, so were all three housed in one place and destroyed? Unlikely!

Things became worse when more copy at the printer's office, stored in a safe for extra protection, was burnt in another attack.

Informal county cricket continued, although Essex's fixtures were curtailed when the county was declared a Defence Area and all travel to it banned. The Lancashire League continued, although all contracts with professionals were

OLD MOORE'S

HOROSCOPE AND ASTRAL DIARY

SAGITTARIUS

foulsham
LONDON • NEW YORK • TORONTO • SYDNEY

W. Foulsham & Co. Ltd
for Foulsham Publishing Ltd
The Old Barrel Store, Drayman's Lane, Marlow, Bucks SL7 2FF

Foulsham books can be found in all good bookshops and direct from
www.foulsham.com

ISBN: 978-0-572-04583-8

Copyright © 2015 Foulsham Publishing Ltd

A CIP record for this book is available from the British Library

Typeset in Great Britain by Chris Brewer Origination, Christchurch
Printed in Great Britain by Martins The Printers, Berwick-upon-Tweed

CONTENTS

INTRODUCTION

Astrology has been a part of life for centuries now, and no matter how technological our lives become, it seems that it never diminishes in popularity. For thousands of years people have been gazing up at the star-clad heavens and seeing their own activities and proclivities reflected in the movement of those little points of light. Across centuries countless hours have been spent studying the way our natures, activities and decisions seem to be paralleled by their predictable movements. Old Moore, a time-served veteran in astrological research, continues to monitor the zodiac and has produced the Astral Diary for 2016, tailor-made to your own astrological makeup.

Old Moore's Astral Diary is unique in its ability to get the heart of your nature and to offer you the sort of advice that might come from a trusted friend. It enables you to see in a day-by-day sense exactly how the planets are working for you. The diary section advises how you can get the best from upcoming situations and allows you to plan ahead successfully. There's also room on each daily entry to record your own observations or appointments.

While other popular astrology books merely deal with your astrological 'Sun sign', the Astral Diaries go much further. Every person on the planet is unique and Old Moore allows you to access your individuality in a number of ways. The front section gives you the chance to work out the placement of the Moon at the time of your birth and to see how its position has set an important seal on your overall nature. Perhaps most important of all, you can use the Astral Diary to discover your Rising Sign. This is the zodiac sign that was appearing over the Eastern horizon at the time of your birth and is just as important to you as an individual as is your Sun sign.

It is the synthesis of many different astrological possibilities that makes you what you are and with the Astral Diaries you can learn so much. How do you react to love and romance? Through the unique Venus tables and the readings that follow them, you can learn where the planet Venus was at the time of your birth. It is even possible to register when little Mercury is 'retrograde', which means that it appears to be moving backwards in space when viewed from the Earth. Mercury rules communication, so be prepared to deal with a few setbacks in this area when you see the sign ☿. The Astral Diary will be an interest and a support throughout the whole year ahead.

Old Moore extends his customary greeting to all people of the Earth and offers his age-old wishes for a happy and prosperous period ahead.

THE ESSENCE
OF SAGITTARIUS

Exploring the Personality of
Sagittarius the Archer

(23RD NOVEMBER – 21ST DECEMBER)

What's in a sign?

Sagittarius is ruled by the large, expansive planet Jupiter, which from an astrological perspective makes all the difference to this happy-go-lucky and very enterprising zodiac sign. This is the sign of the Archer and there is a very good reason for our ancient ancestors having chosen the half-man, half-horse figure with its drawn bow. Not only are Sagittarians fleet-footed like a horse, but the remarks they make, like the arrow, go right to the target.

You love contentious situations and rarely shy away from controversy. With tremendous faith in your own abilities you are not easily kept down, and would usually find it relatively simple to persuade others to follow your course. Though you are born of a Fire sign, you are not as bullying as Aries can be, or as proud as a Leo. Despite this you do have a Fire-sign temper and can be a formidable opponent once you have your dander up.

You rarely choose to take the long route to any destination in life, preferring to drive forward as soon as your mind is made up. Communication comes easy to you and you add to your stock of weapons good intuitive insight and a capacity for brinkmanship that appears to know no bounds. At your best you are earnest, aspiring and honourable, though on the other side of the coin Sagittarians can make the best con artists of all!

What you hate most is to be discouraged, or for others to thwart your intentions. There is a slight tendency for you to use others whilst you are engaging in many of the schemes that are an intrinsic part of your life, though you would never deliberately hurt or offend anyone.

Sagittarian people are natural lovers of fun. When what is required is a shot of enthusiasm, or an immediacy that can cut right through the middle of any red tape, it is the Archer who invariably ends up in charge. When others panic, you come into your own, and you have an ability to get things done in a quarter of the expected time. Whether they are completed perfectly, however, is a different matter altogether.

Sagittarius resources

Sagittarians appear to be the natural conjurors of the zodiac. The stage magician seems to draw objects from thin air, and it often appears that the Archer is able to do something similar. This is an intriguing process to observe, but somewhat difficult to explain. Sagittarians seem to be able to get directly to the heart of any matter, and find it easy to circumnavigate potential difficulties. Thus they achieve objectives that look impossible to observers – hence the conjuring analogy.

Just as the biblical David managed to defeat Goliath with nothing more than a humble pebble and a sling, Sagittarius also goes seemingly naked into battle. The Archer relies on his or her natural wit, together with a fairly instinctive intelligence, a good deal of common sense and a silver tongue. The patient observer must inevitably come to the conclusion that what really matters isn't what the Sagittarian can do, but how much they manage to get others to undertake on their behalf. In other words, people follow your lead without question. This quality can be one of your best resources and only fails when you have doubt about yourself, which fortunately is very rarely.

If other signs could sell refrigerators to Eskimos, you could add a deep-freeze complete with ice tray! This is one of the reasons why so many Archers are engaged in both advertising and marketing. Not only do you know what people want, you also have an instinctive ability to make them want whatever it is you have on offer.

It is likely that you would see nothing remotely mysterious about your ability to peer through to the heart of any matter. In the main you would refer to this as 'gut reaction', despite the fact that it looks distinctly magical to those around you. Fortunately this is part of your mystique, and even if you should choose to take someone for a complete ride, it is doubtful that they would end up disliking you as a result. You don't set out to be considered a genius, and you manage to retain the common touch. This is extremely important, for those with whom you have contacts actively want to help you because you are a 'regular guy'.

Beneath the surface

People tend to be very complicated. Untangling their motives in any given situation is rarely easy. Psychologists have many theories regarding the working of the human psyche and philosophers have struggled with such matters for thousands of years. Clearly none of these people were looking at the zodiac sign of Sagittarius. Ask the average Archer why they did this or that thing and the chances are that you will get a reply something very similar to 'Well, it seemed like a good idea at the time'.

While many people might claim to be uncomplicated, at heart you genuinely are. Complications are something you try to avoid, even though some of your deals in life might look like a roll of barbed wire to those around you. In the main you keep your objectives as simple as possible. This is one of the reasons why it isn't particularly difficult for you to circumnavigate some of the potential pitfalls – you simply won't recognise that they exist. Setting your eyes on the horizon you set off with a jaunty step, refusing to acknowledge problems and, when necessary, sorting them out on the way.

Your general intention is to succeed and this fact permeates just about every facet of your life. Satisfaction doesn't necessarily come for you from a job well done, because the word 'well' in this context often isn't especially important. And when you have one task out of the way, you immediately set your sights on something else. Trying to figure out exactly why you live your life in the way you do, your psychological imperatives and ultimate intentions, costs you too much time, so you probably don't indulge in such idle speculation at all.

You have a warm heart and always want the best for everyone. It almost never occurs to you that other people don't think about things in the way you might and you automatically assume that others will be only too pleased to follow your lead. In the main you are uncomplicated, don't indulge in too many frills and fancies and speak your mind. There really isn't much difference between what you do in life, and what you think about your actions. This is not to infer that you are shallow, merely that you don't see much point in complicating the obvious with too much internal musing.

One of the main reasons why people like you so much is because the 'what you see is what you get' adage is more true in your case than in any other.

Making the best of yourself

Always on the go and invariably looking for a new challenge, it isn't hard to see how Sagittarius makes the best of itself. This is a dynamic, thrusting sign, with a thirst for adventure and a great ability to think on its feet. As a child of Sagittarius you need the cut and thrust of an exciting life in order to show your true mettle. It doesn't do for you to sit around inactive for any length of time and any sort of enforced lay-off is likely to drive you to distraction.

In a career situation your natural proclivities show through, so it's best for you to be in some position which necessitates decision making on a moment-by-moment basis. Production-line work or tasks that involve going over the same ground time and again are not really your forte, though you are certainly not afraid of hard work and can labour on regardless towards any objective – just as long as there is a degree of excitement on the way.

Socially speaking you probably have many friends, and that's the way you like things to be. You need to know that people rate you highly, and will usually be on hand to offer the sort of advice that is always interesting, but probably not totally reasoned. It's a fact that you think everyone has the same ability to think on their feet that typifies your nature, and you trust everyone instinctively – at least once.

In love you need the sort of relationship that allows a degree of personal freedom. You can't be fettered and so have to be your own person under all situations. You are kind and attentive, though sometimes get carried away with the next grand scheme and so you need an understanding partner. Archers should not tie themselves down too early in life and are at their best surrounded by those who love the dynamism and difficult-to-predict qualities exemplified by this zodiac sign.

Most important of all you need to be happy with your lot. Living through restricted or miserable times takes its toll. Fortunately these are few in your life, mainly because of the effort you put into life yourself.

The impressions you give

You must be doing something right because it's a fact that Sagittarius represents one of the most instinctively liked zodiac signs. There are many reasons for this state of affairs. For starters you will always do others a good turn if it's possible. It's true that you are a bit of a rogue on occasions, but that only endears you to the sort of individuals with whom you choose to share your life. You are always the first with a joke, even under difficult circumstances, and you face problems with an open mind and a determination to get through them. On the way you acquire many friends, though in your case many 'acquaintances' might be nearer the mark. This is a situation of your own choosing and though you have so much to recommend you to others, it's a fact that you keep really close ties to the absolute minimum.

Some people might think you rather superficial and perhaps an intellectual lightweight. If so, this only comes about because they don't understand the way your mind works. All the same it is your own nature that leads a few individuals to these conclusions. You can skip from one subject to another, are an insatiable flirt in social situations and love to tell funny stories. 'Depth' isn't really your thing and that means that you could appear to lower the tone of conversations that are getting too heavy for your liking. You do need to be the centre of attention most of the time, which won't exactly endear you to others who have a similar disposition.

People know that you have a temper, like all Fire signs. They will also realise that your outbursts are rare, short-lived and of no real note. You don't bear a grudge and quickly learn that friends are more useful than enemies under any circumstance.

You come across as the capricious, bubbly, lively, likeable child of the zodiac and under such circumstances it would be very difficult for anyone to find fault with you for long. Often outrageous, always interesting and seldom down in the dumps – it's hard to see how you could fail to be loved.

The way forward

It might be best to realise, right from the outset, that you are not indestructible. Deep inside you have all the same insecurities, vulnerabilities and paranoia that the rest of humanity possesses. As a Sagittarian it doesn't do to dwell on such matters, but at least the acknowledgement might stop you going over the edge sometimes. You come from a part of the zodiac that has to be active and which must show itself in the best possible light all the time, and that's a process that is very demanding.

In the main, however, you relish the cut and thrust of life and it is quite likely that you already have the necessary recipe for happiness and success. If you don't, then you are involved in a search that is likely to be both interesting and rewarding, because it isn't really the objective that matters to you but rather the fun you can have on the way.

Be as honest as you can with those around you, though without losing that slightly roguish charm that makes you so appealing. At the same time try to ensure that your own objectives bear others in mind. You can sometimes be a little fickle and, in rare circumstances, unscrupulous. At heart though, you have your own moral convictions and would rarely do anyone a bad turn. On the contrary, you do your best to help those around you, and invariably gain in popularity on the way.

Health-wise you are probably fairly robust but you can run your nervous system into the ground on occasions. There are times when a definite routine suits you physically, but this doesn't always agree with your mental make-up, which is essentially driving and demanding. The peaks and troughs of your life are an inevitable part of what makes you tick, and you would be a poorer person without them.

Explaining yourself is not generally difficult, and neither is the search for personal success, even if you keep looking beyond it to even greater achievements further down the road. Being loved is important, despite the fact that you would deny this on occasions. Perhaps you don't always know yourself as well as you might, though since you are not an inveterate deep thinker it is likely that this is not a problem to you.

If you are already an adult, it's likely the path you are presently following is the one for you. That doesn't mean to say that you will keep to it, or find it universally rewarding. You find new promise in each day, and that's the joy of Sagittarius.

SAGITTARIUS ON THE CUSP

Old Moore is often asked how astrological profiles are altered for those people born at either the beginning or the end of a zodiac sign, or, more properly, on the cusps of a sign. In the case of Sagittarius this would be on the 23rd of November and for two or three days after, and similarly at the end of the sign, probably from the 19th to the 21st of December. In this year's Astral Diaries, once again, Old Moore sets out to explain the differences regarding cuspid signs.

The Scorpio Cusp – November 23rd to 25th

You could turn out to be one of the most well-liked people around, especially if you draw heavily from the more positive qualities of the two zodiac signs that have the most profound part to play in your life. Taken alone the Sagittarian is often accused of being rather too flighty. Sagittarians are often guilty of flirting and sometimes fall foul of people who take a more serious view of life in general. The presence in your make-up of the much deeper and more contemplative sign of Scorpio brings a quiet and a sense of reserve that the Sagittarian nature sometimes lacks. Although you like to have a good time and would be more than willing to dance the night away, you are probably also happy enough when the time comes to go home. Family means much to you and you have a great sensitivity to the needs of those around you. What makes all the difference is that you not only understand others, but you have the potential to take practical steps to help them.

You are probably not quite the workaholic that the Archer alone tends to be and can gain rest and relaxation, which has to be good for you in the longer term. You don't lack the ability to be successful but your level of application is considered, less frenetic and altogether more ordered. It's true that some confusion comes into your life from time to time, but you have the resources to deal with such eventualities, and you do so with a smile on your face most of the time. People would warm to you almost instantly and you are likely to do whatever you can to support family members and friends.

Often sinking into a dream world if you feel threatened, some of the achievements that are second nature to the Sagittarian are left on the shelf for a while. There are times when this turns out to be a blessing, if only because your actions are more considered. Personality clashes with others are less likely with this combination and Sagittarius also modifies the slightly moody qualities that come with Scorpio alone. More methodical in every way than the usual Archer, in many situations you are a good combination of optimist and pessimist.

The Capricorn Cusp – December 19th to 21st

The fact that comes across almost immediately with the Capricorn cusp of Sagittarius is how very practical you tend to be. Most of you would be ideal company on a desert island, for a number of reasons. Firstly you are quite self-contained, which Sagittarius taken alone certainly is not. You would soon get your head round the practical difficulties of finding food and shelter, and would be very happy to provide these necessities for your companions too. Unlike the typical Sagittarian you do not boast and probably do not come across as being quite so overbearing as the Archer seems to be. For all this you are friendly, chatty, love to meet many different and interesting types and do whatever you can to be of assistance to a world which is all the better for having you in it.

There is less of a tendency for you to worry at a superficial level than Sagittarius alone is inclined to do, mainly because long periods of practical application bring with them a contemplative tendency that Sagittarius sometimes lacks. In love you tend to be quite sincere, even if the slightly fickle tendencies of the Archer do show through now and again. Any jealousy that is levelled at you by your partner could be as a result of your natural attractiveness, which you probably don't seek. Fairly comfortable in almost any sort of company, you are at your best when faced with individuals who have something intelligent and interesting to say. As a salesperson you would be second to none, but it would be essential for you to believe absolutely in the product or service you were selling.

Almost any sort of work is possible in your case, though you wouldn't take too kindly to being restricted in any way, and need the chance to show what your practical nature is worth, as well as your keen perception and organisational abilities. What matters most for you at work is that you are well liked by others and that you manage to maintain a position of control through inspiring confidence. On a creative level, the combination of Sagittarius and Capricorn would make you a good sculptor, or possibly a natural landscape gardener.

SAGITTARIUS AND ITS ASCENDANTS

The nature of every individual on the planet is composed of the rich variety of zodiac signs and planetary positions that were present at the time of their birth. Your Sun sign, which in your case is Sagittarius, is one of the many factors when it comes to assessing the unique person you are. Probably the most important consideration, other than your Sun sign, is to establish the zodiac sign that was rising over the eastern horizon at the time that you were born. This is your Ascending or Rising sign. Most popular astrology fails to take account of the Ascendant, and yet its importance remains with you from the very moment of your birth, through every day of your life. The Ascendant is evident in the way you approach the world, and so, when meeting a person for the first time, it is this astrological influence that you are most likely to notice first. Our Ascending sign essentially represents what we appear to be, while the Sun sign is what we feel inside ourselves.

The Ascendant also has the potential for modifying our overall nature. For example, if you were born at a time of day when Sagittarius was passing over the eastern horizon (this would be around the time of dawn) then you would be classed as a double Sagittarius. As such, you would typify this zodiac sign, both internally and in your dealings with others. However, if your Ascendant sign turned out to be an Earth sign, such as Taurus, there would be a profound alteration of nature, away from the expected qualities of Sagittarius.

One of the reasons why popular astrology often ignores the Ascendant is that it has always been rather difficult to establish. Old Moore has found a way to make this possible by devising an easy-to-use table, which you will find on page 125 of this book. Using this, you can establish your Ascendant sign at a glance. You will need to know your rough time of birth, then it is simply a case of following the instructions.

For those readers who have no idea of their time of birth it might be worth allowing a good friend, or perhaps your partner, to read through the section that follows this introduction. Someone who deals with you on a regular basis may easily discover your Ascending sign, even though you could have some difficulty establishing it for yourself. A good understanding of this component of your nature is essential if you want to be aware of that 'other person' who is responsible for the way you make contact with the world at large. Your Sun sign, Ascendant sign, and the other pointers in this book will, together, allow you a far better understanding of what makes you tick as an individual. Peeling back the different layers of your astrological make-up can be an enlightening experience, and the Ascendant may represent one of the most important layers of all.

Sagittarius with Sagittarius Ascendant

You are very easy to spot, even in a crowd. There is hardly a more dynamic individual to be found anywhere in the length and breadth of the zodiac. You know what you want from life and have a pretty good idea about how you will get it. The fact that you are always so cocksure is a source of great wonder to those around you, but they can't see deep inside, where you are not half as certain as you appear to be. In the main you show yourself to be kind, attentive, caring and a loyal friend. To balance this, you are determined and won't be thwarted by anything.

You keep up a searing pace through life and sometimes find it difficult to understand those people who have slightly less energy. In your better moments you understand that you are unique and will wait for others to catch up. Quite often you need periods of rest in order to recharge batteries that run down through over-use, but it doesn't take you too long to get yourself back on top form. In matters of the heart you can be slightly capricious, but you are a confident lover who knows the right words and gestures. If you are ever accused of taking others for granted you might need to indulge in some self-analysis.

Sagittarius with Capricorn Ascendant

The typical Sagittarian nature is modified for the better when Capricorn is part of the deal. It's true that you manage to push forward progressively under most circumstances, but you also possess staying power and can work long and hard to achieve your objectives, most of which are carefully planned in advance. Few people have the true measure of your nature, for it runs rather deeper than appears to be the case on the surface. Routines don't bother you as much as would be the case for Sagittarius when taken alone, and you don't care if any objective takes weeks, months or even years to achieve. You are very fond of those you take to, and prove to be a capable friend, even when things get tough.

In love relationships you are steadfast and reliable, and yet you never lose the ability to entertain. Yours is a dry sense of humour which shows itself to a multitude of different people and which doesn't evaporate, even on those occasions when life gets tough. It might take you a long time to find the love of your life, but when you do there is a greater possibility of retaining the relationship for a long period. You don't tend to inherit money, but you can easily make it for yourself, though you don't worry too much about the amount. On the whole you are self-sufficient and sensible.

Sagittarius with Aquarius Ascendant

There is an original streak to your nature which is very attractive to the people with whom you share your life. Always different, ever on the go and anxious to try out the next experiment in life, you are interested in almost everything and yet deeply attached to almost nothing. Everyone you know thinks that you are a little 'odd', but you probably don't mind them believing this because you know it to be true. In fact it is possible that you positively relish your eccentricity, which sets you apart from the common herd and means that you are always going to be noticed.

Although it may seem strange with this combination of Air and Fire, you can be distinctly cool on occasions, have a deep and abiding love of your own company now and again, and won't easily be understood. Love comes fairly easily to you but there are times when you are accused of being self-possessed, self-indulgent and not willing enough to fall in line with the wishes of those around you. Despite this you walk on and on down your own path. At heart you are an extrovert and you love to party, often late into the night. Luxury appeals to you, though it tends to be of the transient sort. Travel could easily play a major and a very important part in your life.

Sagittarius with Pisces Ascendant

A very attractive combination this, because the more dominant qualities of the Archer are somehow mellowed-out by the caring Water-sign qualities of the Fishes. You can be very outgoing, but there is always a deeper side to your nature that allows others to know that you are thinking about them. Few people could fall out with either your basic nature or your attitude to the world at large, even though there are depths to your personality that may not be easily understood. You are capable, have a good executive ability and can work hard to achieve your objectives, even if you get a little disillusioned on the way. Much of your life is given over to helping those around you and there is a great tendency for you to work for and on behalf of humanity as a whole. A sense of community is brought to most of what you do and you enjoy co-operation.

Although you have the natural Sagittarian ability to attract people to you, the Pisces half of your nature makes you just a little more reserved in personal matters than might otherwise be the case. More careful in your choices than either sign taken alone, you still have to make certain that your motivations when commencing a personal relationship are the right ones. You love to be happy, and to offer gifts of happiness to others.

Sagittarius with Aries Ascendant

What a lovely combination this can be, for the devil-may-care aspects of Sagittarius lighten the load of a sometimes too serious Aries interior. Everything that glistens is not gold, though it's hard to convince you of the fact because, to mix metaphors, you can make a silk purse out of a sow's ear. Almost everyone loves you, and in return you offer a friendship that is warm and protective, but not as demanding as sometimes tends to be the case with the Aries type. Relationships may be many and varied and there is often more than one major attachment in the life of those holding this combination. You can bring a breath of spring to any relationship, though you need to ensure that the person concerned is capable of keeping up with the hectic pace of your life.

It may appear from time to time that you are rather too trusting for your own good, though deep inside you are very astute, and it seems that almost everything you undertake works out well in the end. This has nothing to do with native luck and is really down to the fact that you are much more calculating than might appear to be the case at first sight. As a parent you are protective, yet offer sufficient room for self-expression.

Sagittarius with Taurus Ascendant

A dual nature is evident here, and if it doesn't serve to confuse you it will certainly be a cause of concern to many of the people with whom you share your life. You like to have a good time and are a natural party-goer. On such occasions you are accommodating, chatty and good to know. But contrast this with the quieter side of Taurus, which is directly opposed to your Sagittarian qualities. The opposition of forces is easy for you to deal with because you inhabit your own body and mind all the time, but it's far less easy for friends and relatives to understand. As a result, on those occasions when you decide that, socially speaking, enough is enough, you will need to explain the fact to the twelve people who are waiting outside your door with party hats and whoopee cushions.

Confidence to do almost anything is not far from the forefront of your mind and you readily embark on adventures that would have some types flapping about in horror. Here again, it is important to realise that we are not all built the same way and that gentle coaxing is sometimes necessary to bring others round to your point of view. If you really have a fault, it could be that you are so busy being your own, rather less than predictable self, that you fail to take the rest of the world into account.

Sagittarius with Gemini Ascendant

'Tomorrow is another day!' This is your belief and you stick to it. There isn't a brighter and more optimistic soul to be found than you and almost everyone you come into contact with is touched by the fact. Dashing about from one place to another, you manage to get more things done in one day than most other people would achieve in a week. Of course this explains why you are so likely to wear yourself out and it means that frequent periods of absolute rest are necessary if you are to remain truly healthy and happy. Sagittarius makes you brave and sometimes a little headstrong, so you need to curb your natural enthusiasm while you stop to think about the consequences of your actions.

It's not really certain if you do 'think' in the accepted sense of the word, because the lightning qualities of both these signs mean that your reactions are second to none. However, you are not indestructible and you put far more pressure on yourself than would often be sensible. Routines are not your thing at all, and many of you manage to hold down two or more jobs at once. It might be an idea to stop and smell the flowers on the way, and you could certainly do with putting your feet up much more than you do. However, you probably won't still be reading this passage because you will have something far more important to do!

Sagittarius with Cancer Ascendant

You have far more drive, enthusiasm and get-up-and-go than would seem to be the case for Cancer when taken alone, but all of this is tempered with a certain quiet compassion that probably makes you the best sort of Sagittarian too. It's true that you don't like to be on your own or to retire in your shell quite as much as the Crab usually does, though there are, even in your case, occasions when this is going to be necessary. Absolute concentration can sometimes be a problem to you, though this is hardly likely to be the case when you are dealing with matters relating to your home or family, both of which reign supreme in your thinking. Always loving and kind, you are a social animal and enjoy being out there in the real world, expressing the deeper opinions of Cancer much more readily than would often be the case with other combinations relating to the sign of the Crab.

Personality is not lacking and you tend to be very popular, not least because you are the fountain of good and practical advice. You want to get things done and retain a practical approach to most situations which is the envy of many other people. As a parent you are second to none, combining common sense, dignity and a sensible approach. To balance this you stay young enough to understand children.

Sagittarius with Leo Ascendant

Above and beyond anything else you are naturally funny, and this is an aspect of your nature that will bring you intact through a whole series of problems that you manage to create for yourself. Chatty, witty, charming, kind and loving, you personify the best qualities of both these signs, whilst also retaining the Fire-sign ability to keep going, long after the rest of the party has gone home to bed. Being great fun to have around, you attract friends in the way that a magnet attracts iron filings. Many of these will be casual connections but there will always be a nucleus of deep, abiding attachments that may stay around you for most of your life.

You don't often suffer from fatigue, but on those occasions when you do there is ample reason to stay still for a while and to take stock of situations. Routines are not your thing and you like to fill your life with variety. It's important to do certain things right, however, and staying power is something that comes with age, assisted by the Fixed quality of Leo. Few would lock horns with you in an argument, which you always have to win. In a way you are a natural debator but you can sometimes carry things too far if you are up against a worthy opponent. You have the confidence to sail through situations that would defeat others.

Sagittarius with Virgo Ascendant

This is a combination that might look rather odd at first sight because these two signs have so very little in common. However, the saying goes that opposites attract, and in terms of the personality you display to the world this is especially true in your case. Not everyone understands what makes you tick but you try to show the least complicated face to the world that you can manage to display. You can be deep and secretive on occasions, and yet at other times you can start talking as soon as you climb out of bed and never stop until you are back there again. Inspirational and spontaneous, you take the world by storm on those occasions when you are free from worries and firing on all cylinders. It is a fact that you support your friends, though there are rather more of them than would be the case for Virgo taken on its own, and you don't always choose them as wisely as you might.

There are times when you display a temper, and although Sagittarius is incapable of bearing a grudge, the same cannot be said for Virgo, which has a better memory than the elephant. For the best results in life you need to relax as much as possible and avoid overheating that powerful and busy brain. Virgo gives you the ability to concentrate on one thing at once, a skill you should encourage.

Sagittarius with Libra Ascendant

A very happy combination this, with a great desire for life in all its forms and a need to push forward the bounds of the possible in a way that few other zodiac sign connections would do. You don't like the unpleasant or ugly in life and yet you are capable of dealing with both if you have to. Giving so much to humanity, you still manage to retain a degree of individuality that would surprise many, charm others, and please all.

On the reverse side of the same coin you might find that you are sometimes accused of being fickle, but this is only an expression of your need for change and variety, which is intrinsic to both these signs. True, you have more of a temper than would be the case for Libra when taken on its own, but such incidents would see you up and down in a flash and it is almost impossible for you to bear a grudge of any sort. Routines get on your nerves and you are far happier when you can please yourself and get ahead at your own pace, which is quite fast.

As a lover you can make a big impression and most of you will not go short of affection in the early days, before you choose to commit yourself. Once you do, there is always a chance of romantic problems, but these are less likely when you have chosen carefully in the first place.

Sagittarius with Scorpio Ascendant

There are many gains with this combination, and most of you reading this will already be familiar with the majority of them. Sagittarius offers a bright and hopeful approach to life, but may not always have the staying power and the patience to get what it really needs. Scorpio, on the other hand, can be too deep for its own good, is very self-seeking on occasions and extremely giving to others. Both the signs have problems when taken on their own, and, it has to be said, double the difficulties when they come together. But this is not usually the case. Invariably the presence of Scorpio slows down the over-quick responses of the Archer, whilst the inclusion of Sagittarius prevents Scorpio from taking itself too seriously.

Life is so often a game of extremes, when all the great spiritual masters of humanity have indicated that a 'middle way' is the path to choose. You have just the right combination of skills and mental faculties to find that elusive path, and can bring great joy to yourself and others as a result. Most of the time you are happy, optimistic, helpful and a joy to know. You have mental agility, backed up by a stunning intuition, which itself would rarely let you down. Keep a sense of proportion and understand that your depth of intellect is necessary in order to curb the more flighty aspects of Scorpio.

THE MOON AND THE PART IT PLAYS IN YOUR LIFE

In astrology the Moon is probably the single most important heavenly body after the Sun. Its unique position, as partner to the Earth on its journey around the solar system, means that the Moon appears to pass through the signs of the zodiac extremely quickly. The zodiac position of the Moon at the time of your birth plays a great part in personal character and is especially significant in the build-up of your emotional nature.

Sun Moon Cycles

The first lunar cycle deals with the part the position of the Moon plays relative to your Sun sign. I have made the fluctuations of this pattern easy for you to understand by means of a simple cyclic graph. It appears on the first page of each 'Your Month At A Glance', under the title 'Highs and Lows'. The graph displays the lunar cycle and you will soon learn to understand how its movements have a bearing on your level of energy and your abilities.

Your Own Moon Sign

Discovering the position of the Moon at the time of your birth has always been notoriously difficult because tracking the complex zodiac positions of the Moon is not easy. This process has been reduced to three simple stages with Old Moore's unique Lunar Tables. A breakdown of the Moon's zodiac positions can be found from page 28 onwards, so that once you know what your Moon Sign is, you can see what part this plays in the overall build-up of your personal character.

If you follow the instructions on the next page you will soon be able to work out exactly what zodiac sign the Moon occupied on the day that you were born and you can then go on to compare the reading for this position with those of your Sun sign and your Ascendant. It is partly the comparison between these three important positions that goes towards making you the unique individual you are.

HOW TO DISCOVER YOUR MOON SIGN

This is a three-stage process. You may need a pen and a piece of paper but if you follow the instructions below the process should only take a minute or so.

STAGE 1 First of all you need to know the Moon Age at the time of your birth. If you look at Moon Table 1, on page 26, you will find all the years between 1918 and 2016 down the left side. Find the year of your birth and then trace across to the right to the month of your birth. Where the two intersect you will find a number. This is the date of the New Moon in the month that you were born. You now need to count forward the number of days between the New Moon and your own birthday. For example, if the New Moon in the month of your birth was shown as being the 6th and you were born on the 20th, your Moon Age Day would be 14. If the New Moon in the month of your birth came after your birthday, you need to count forward from the New Moon in the previous month. If you were born in a Leap Year, remember to count the 29th February. You can tell if your birth year was a Leap Year if the last two digits can be divided by four. Whatever the result, jot this number down so that you do not forget it.

STAGE 2 Take a look at Moon Table 2 on page 27. Down the left hand column look for the date of your birth. Now trace across to the month of your birth. Where the two meet you will find a letter. Copy this letter down alongside your Moon Age Day.

STAGE 3 Moon Table 3 on page 27 will supply you with the zodiac sign the Moon occupied on the day of your birth. Look for your Moon Age Day down the left hand column and then for the letter you found in Stage 2. Where the two converge you will find a zodiac sign and this is the sign occupied by the Moon on the day that you were born.

Your Zodiac Moon Sign Explained

You will find a profile of all zodiac Moon Signs on pages 28 to 31, showing in yet another way how astrology helps to make you into the individual that you are. In each daily entry of the Astral Diary you can find the zodiac position of the Moon for every day of the year. This also allows you to discover your lunar birthdays. Since the Moon passes through all the signs of the zodiac in about a month, you can expect something like twelve lunar birthdays each year. At these times you are likely to be emotionally steady and able to make the sort of decisions that have real, lasting value.

Moon Table 1

YEAR	OCT	NOV	DEC
1918	4	3	2
1919	23	22	21
1920	12	10	10
1921	1/30	29	29
1922	20	19	18
1923	10	8	8
1924	28	26	26
1925	17	16	15
1926	6	5	5
1927	25	24	24
1928	14	12	12
1929	2	1	1/30
1930	20	19	19
1931	11	9	9
1932	29	27	27
1933	19	17	17
1934	8	7	6
1935	27	26	25
1936	15	14	13
1937	4	3	2
1938	23	22	21
1939	12	11	10
1940	1/30	29	28
1941	20	19	18
1942	10	8	8
1943	29	27	27
1944	17	15	15
1945	6	4	4
1946	24	23	23
1947	14	12	12
1948	2	1	1/30
1949	21	20	19
1950	11	9	9

YEAR	OCT	NOV	DEC
1951	1/30	29	28
1952	18	17	17
1953	8	6	6
1954	26	25	25
1955	15	14	14
1956	4	2	2
1957	23	21	21
1958	12	11	10
1959	2/31	30	29
1960	20	19	18
1961	9	8	7
1962	28	27	26
1963	17	15	15
1964	5	4	4
1965	24	22	22
1966	14	12	12
1967	3	2	1/30
1968	22	21	20
1969	10	9	9
1970	1/30	29	28
1971	19	18	17
1972	8	6	6
1973	26	25	25
1974	15	14	14
1975	5	3	3
1976	23	21	21
1977	12	11	10
1978	2/31	30	29
1979	20	19	18
1980	9	8	7
1981	27	26	26
1982	17	15	15
1983	6	4	4

YEAR	OCT	NOV	DEC
1984	24	22	22
1985	14	12	12
1986	3	2	1/30
1987	22	21	20
1988	10	9	9
1989	29	28	28
1990	18	17	17
1991	8	6	6
1992	25	24	24
1993	15	14	14
1994	5	3	2
1995	24	22	22
1996	11	10	10
1997	31	30	29
1998	20	19	18
1999	8	8	7
2000	27	26	25
2001	17	16	15
2002	6	4	4
2003	25	24	23
2004	12	11	11
2005	2	1	1/31
2006	21	20	20
2007	11	9	9
2008	29	28	27
2009	18	17	16
2010	8	8	6
2011	27	25	25
2012	15	13	12
2013	4	2	2
2014	22	22	1
2015	12	11	20
2016	30	29	29

Table 2

DAY	NOV	DEC
1	e	i
2	e	i
3	e	m
4	f	m
5	f	n
6	f	n
7	f	n
8	f	n
9	f	n
10	f	n
11	f	n
12	f	n
13	g	n
14	g	n
15	g	n
16	g	n
17	g	n
18	g	n
19	g	n
20	g	n
21	g	n
22	g	n
23	i	q
24	i	q
25	i	q
26	i	q
27	i	q
28	i	q
29	i	q
30	i	q
31	–	q

Table 3

M/D	e	f	g	i	m	n	q
0	SC	SC	SC	SA	SA	SA	CP
1	SC	SC	SA	SA	SA	CP	CP
2	SC	SA	SA	CP	CP	CP	AQ
3	SA	SA	CP	CP	CP	AQ	AQ
4	SA	CP	CP	CP	AQ	AQ	PI
5	CP	CP	AQ	AQ	AQ	PI	PI
6	CP	AQ	AQ	AQ	AQ	PI	AR
7	AQ	AQ	PI	PI	PI	AR	AR
8	AQ	PI	PI	PI	PI	AR	AR
9	AQ	PI	PI	AR	AR	TA	TA
10	PI	AR	AR	AR	AR	TA	TA
11	PI	AR	AR	TA	TA	TA	GE
12	AR	TA	TA	TA	TA	GE	GE
13	AR	TA	TA	GE	GE	GE	GE
14	TA	GE	GE	GE	GE	CA	CA
15	TA	TA	TA	GE	GE	GE	CA
16	TA	GE	GE	GE	CA	CA	CA
17	GE	GE	GE	CA	CA	CA	LE
18	GE	GE	CA	CA	CA	LE	LE
19	GE	CA	CA	CA	LE	LE	LE
20	CA	CA	CA	LE	LE	LE	VI
21	CA	CA	LE	LE	LE	VI	VI
22	CA	LE	LE	VI	VI	VI	LI
23	LE	LE	LE	VI	VI	VI	LI
24	LE	LE	VI	VI	VI	LI	LI
25	LE	VI	VI	LI	LI	LI	SC
26	VI	VI	LI	LI	LI	SC	SC
27	VI	LI	LI	SC	SC	SC	SA
28	LI	LI	LI	SC	SC	SC	SA
29	LI	LI	SC	SC	SA	SA	SA

AR = Aries, TA = Taurus, GE = Gemini, CA = Cancer, LE = Leo, VI = Virgo, LI = Libra, SC = Scorpio, SA = Sagittarius, CP = Capricorn, AQ = Aquarius, PI = Pisces

MOON SIGNS

Moon in Aries

You have a strong imagination, courage, determination and a desire to do things in your own way and forge your own path through life.

Originality is a key attribute; you are seldom stuck for ideas although your mind is changeable and you could take the time to focus on individual tasks. Often quick-tempered, you take orders from few people and live life at a fast pace. Avoid health problems by taking regular time out for rest and relaxation.

Emotionally, it is important that you talk to those you are closest to and work out your true feelings. Once you discover that people are there to help, there is less necessity for you to do everything yourself.

Moon in Taurus

The Moon in Taurus gives you a courteous and friendly manner, which means you are likely to have many friends.

The good things in life mean a lot to you, as Taurus is an Earth sign that delights in experiences which please the senses. Hence you are probably a lover of good food and drink, which may in turn mean you need to keep an eye on the bathroom scales, especially as looking good is also important to you.

Emotionally you are fairly stable and you stick by your own standards. Taureans do not respond well to change. Intuition also plays an important part in your life.

Moon in Gemini

You have a warm-hearted character, sympathetic and eager to help others. At times reserved, you can also be articulate and chatty: this is part of the paradox of Gemini, which always brings duplicity to the nature. You are interested in current affairs, have a good intellect, and are good company and likely to have many friends. Most of your friends have a high opinion of you and would be ready to defend you should the need arise. However, this is usually unnecessary, as you are quite capable of defending yourself in any verbal confrontation.

Travel is important to your inquisitive mind and you find intellectual stimulus in mixing with people from different cultures. You also gain much from reading, writing and the arts but you do need plenty of rest and relaxation in order to avoid fatigue.

Moon in Cancer

The Moon in Cancer at the time of birth is a fortunate position as Cancer is the Moon's natural home. This means that the qualities of compassion and understanding given by the Moon are especially enhanced in your nature, and you are friendly and sociable and cope well with emotional pressures. You cherish home and family life, and happily do the domestic tasks. Your surroundings are important to you and you hate squalor and filth. You are likely to have a love of music and poetry.

Your basic character, although at times changeable like the Moon itself, depends on symmetry. You aim to make your surroundings comfortable and harmonious, for yourself and those close to you.

Moon in Leo

The best qualities of the Moon and Leo come together to make you warmhearted, fair, ambitious and self-confident. With good organisational abilities, you invariably rise to a position of responsibility in your chosen career. This is fortunate as you don't enjoy being an 'also-ran' and would rather be an important part of a small organisation than a menial in a large one.

You should be lucky in love, and happy, provided you put in the effort to make a comfortable home for yourself and those close to you. It is likely that you will have a love of pleasure, sport, music and literature. Life brings you many rewards, most of them as a direct result of your own efforts, although you may be luckier than average and ready to make the best of any situation.

Moon in Virgo

You are endowed with good mental abilities and a keen receptive memory, but you are never ostentatious or pretentious. Naturally quite reserved, you still have many friends, especially of the opposite sex. Marital relationships must be discussed carefully and worked at so that they remain harmonious, as personal attachments can be a problem if you do not give them your full attention.

Talented and persevering, you possess artistic qualities and are a good homemaker. Earning your honours through genuine merit, you work long and hard towards your objectives but show little pride in your achievements. Many short journeys will be undertaken in your life.

Moon in Libra

With the Moon in Libra you are naturally popular and make friends easily. People like you, probably more than you realise, you bring fun to a party and are a natural diplomat. For all its good points, Libra is not the most stable of astrological signs and, as a result, your emotions can be a little unstable too. Therefore, although the Moon in Libra is said to be good for love and marriage, your Sun sign and Rising sign will have an important effect on your emotional and loving qualities.

You must remember to relate to others in your decision-making. Co-operation is crucial because Libra represents the 'balance' of life that can only be achieved through harmonious relationships. Conformity is not easy for you because Libra, an Air sign, likes its independence.

Moon in Scorpio

Some people might call you pushy. In fact, all you really want to do is to live life to the full and protect yourself and your family from the pressures of life. Take care to avoid giving the impression of being sarcastic or impulsive and use your energies wisely and constructively.

You have great courage and you invariably achieve your goals by force of personality and sheer effort. You are fond of mystery and are good at predicting the outcome of situations and events. Travel experiences can be beneficial to you.

You may experience problems if you do not take time to examine your motives in a relationship, and also if you allow jealousy, always a feature of Scorpio, to cloud your judgement.

Moon in Sagittarius

The Moon in Sagittarius helps to make you a generous individual with humanitarian qualities and a kind heart. Restlessness may be intrinsic as your mind is seldom still. Perhaps because of this, you have a need for change that could lead you to several major moves during your adult life. You are not afraid to stand your ground when you know your judgement is right, you speak directly and have good intuition.

At work you are quick, efficient and versatile and so you make an ideal employee. You need work to be intellectually demanding and do not enjoy tedious routines.

In relationships, you anger quickly if faced with stupidity or deception, though you are just as quick to forgive and forget. Emotionally, there are times when your heart rules your head.

Moon in Capricorn

The Moon in Capricorn makes you popular and likely to come into the public eye in some way. The watery Moon is not entirely comfortable in the Earth sign of Capricorn and this may lead to some difficulties in the early years of life. An initial lack of creative ability and indecision must be overcome before the true qualities of patience and perseverance inherent in Capricorn can show through.

You have good administrative ability and are a capable worker, and if you are careful you can accumulate wealth. But you must be cautious and take professional advice in partnerships, as you are open to deception. You may be interested in social or welfare work, which suit your organisational skills and sympathy for others.

Moon in Aquarius

The Moon in Aquarius makes you an active and agreeable person with a friendly, easy-going nature. Sympathetic to the needs of others, you flourish in a laid-back atmosphere. You are broad-minded, fair and open to suggestion, although sometimes you have an unconventional quality which others can find hard to understand.

You are interested in the strange and curious, and in old articles and places. You enjoy trips to these places and gain much from them. Political, scientific and educational work interests you and you might choose a career in science or technology.

Money-wise, you make gains through innovation and concentration and Lunar Aquarians often tackle more than one job at a time. In love you are kind and honest.

Moon in Pisces

You have a kind, sympathetic nature, somewhat retiring at times, but you always take account of others' feelings and help when you can.

Personal relationships may be problematic, but as life goes on you can learn from your experiences and develop a better understanding of yourself and the world around you.

You have a fondness for travel, appreciate beauty and harmony and hate disorder and strife. You may be fond of literature and would make a good writer or speaker yourself. You have a creative imagination and may come across as an incurable romantic. You have strong intuition, maybe bordering on a mediumistic quality, which sets you apart from the mass. You may not be rich in cash terms, but your personal gifts are worth more than gold.

SAGITTARIUS IN LOVE

Discover how compatible in love you are with people from the same and other signs of the zodiac. Five stars equals a match made in heaven!

Sagittarius meets Sagittarius

Although perhaps not the very best partnership for Sagittarius, this must rank as one of the most eventful, electrifying and interesting of the bunch. They will think alike, which is often the key to any relationship but, unfortunately, they may be so busy leading their own lives that they don't spend much time together. Their social life should be something special, and there could be lots of travel. However, domestic responsibilities need to be carefully shared and the family might benefit from a helping hand in this area. Star rating: ****

Sagittarius meets Capricorn

Any real problem here will stem from a lack of understanding. Capricorn is very practical and needs to be constantly on the go, though in a fairly low-key sort of way. Sagittarius is busy too, though always in a panic and invariably behind its deadlines, which will annoy organised Capricorn. Sagittarius doesn't really have the depth of nature that best suits an Earth sign like Capricorn and its flirty nature could upset the sensitive Goat, though its lighter attitude could be cheering, too. Star rating: ***

Sagittarius meets Aquarius

Both Sagittarius and Aquarius are into mind games, which may lead to something of an intellectual competition. If one side is happy to be bamboozled it won't be a problem, but it is more likely that the relationship will turn into a competition which won't auger well for its long-term future. However, on the plus side, both signs are adventurous and sociable, so as long as there is always something new and interesting to do, the match could end up turning out very well. Star rating: **

Sagittarius meets Pisces

Probably the least likely success story for either sign, which is why it scores so low on the star rating. The basic problem is an almost total lack of understanding. A successful relationship needs empathy and progress towards a shared goal but, although both are eager to please, Pisces is too deep and Sagittarius too flighty – they just don't belong on the same planet! As pals, they have more in common and so a friendship is the best hope of success and happiness. Star rating: *

Sagittarius meets Aries

This can be one of the most favourable matches of them all. Both Aries and Sagittarius are Fire signs, which often leads to clashes of will, but this pair find a mutual understanding. Sagittarius helps Aries to develop a better sense of humour, while Aries teaches the Archer about consistency on the road to success. Some patience is called for on both sides, but these people have a natural liking for each other. Add this to growing love and you have a long-lasting combination that is hard to beat. Star rating: *****

Sagittarius meets Taurus

On first impression, Taurus may not like Sagittarius, which may seem brash, and even common, when viewed through the Bull's refined eyes. But, there is hope of success because the two signs have so much to offer each other. The Archer is enthralled by the Taurean's natural poise and beauty, while Taurus always needs more basic confidence, which is no problem to Sagittarius who has plenty to spare. Both signs love to travel. There are certain to be ups and downs, but that doesn't prevent an interesting, inspiring and even exciting combination. Star rating: ***

Sagittarius meets Gemini

A paradoxical relationship this. On paper, the two signs have much in common, but unfortunately, they are often so alike that life turns into a fiercely fought competition. Both signs love change and diversity and both want to be the life and soul of the party. But in life there must always be a leader and a follower, and neither of this pair wants to be second. Both also share a tendency towards infidelity, which may develop into a problem as time passes. This could be an interesting match, but not necessarily successful. Star rating: **

Sagittarius meets Cancer

Although probably not an immediate success, there is hope for this couple. It's hard to see how this pair could get together, because they have few mutual interests. Sagittarius is always on the go, loves a hectic social life and dances the night away. Cancer prefers the cinema or a concert. But, having met, Cancer will appreciate the Archer's happy and cheerful nature, while Sagittarius finds Cancer alluring and intriguing and, as the saying goes, opposites attract. A long-term relationship would focus on commitment to family, with Cancer leading this area. Star rating: ***

Sagittarius meets Leo

An excellent match as Leo and Sagittarius have so much in common. Their general approach to life is very similar, although as they are both Fire signs they can clash impressively! Sagittarius is shallower and more flippant than Leo likes to think of itself, and the Archer will be the one taking emotional chances. Sagittarius has met its match in the Lion's den, as brave Leo won't be outdone by anyone. Financially, they will either be very wealthy or struggling, and family life may be chaotic. Problems, like joys, are handled jointly – and that leads to happiness. Star rating: *****

Sagittarius meets Virgo

There can be some quite strange happenings inside this relationship. Sagittarius and Virgo view life so differently there are always new discoveries. Virgo is much more of a home-bird than Sagittarius, but that won't matter if the Archer introduces its hectic social life gradually. More importantly, Sagittarius understands that it takes Virgo a long time to free its hidden 'inner sprite', but once free it will be fun all the way – until Virgo's thrifty nature takes over. There are great possibilities, but effort is required. Star rating: ★★★

Sagittarius meets Libra

Libra and Sagittarius are both adaptable signs who get on well with most people, but this promising outlook often does not follow through because each brings out the 'flighty' side of the other. This combination is great for a fling, but when the romance is over someone needs to see to the practical side of life. Both signs are well meaning, pleasant and kind, but are either of them constant enough to build a life together? In at least some cases, the answer would be no. Star rating: ★★★

Sagittarius meets Scorpio

Sagittarius needs constant stimulation and loves to be busy from dawn till dusk which may mean that it feels rather frustrated by Scorpio. Scorpions are hard workers, too, but they are also contemplative and need periods of quiet which may mean that they appear dull to Sagittarius. This could lead to a gulf between the two which must be overcome. With time and patience on both sides, this can be a lucrative encounter and good in terms of home and family. A variable alliance. Star rating: ★★★

VENUS:
THE PLANET OF LOVE

If you look up at the sky around sunset or sunrise you will often see Venus in close attendance to the Sun. It is arguably one of the most beautiful sights of all and there is little wonder that historically it became associated with the goddess of love. But although Venus does play an important part in the way you view love and in the way others see you romantically, this is only one of the spheres of influence that it enjoys in your overall character.

Venus has a part to play in the more cultured side of your life and has much to do with your appreciation of art, literature, music and general creativity. Even the way you look is responsive to the part of the zodiac that Venus occupied at the start of your life, though this fact is also down to your Sun sign and Ascending sign. If, at the time you were born, Venus occupied one of the more gregarious zodiac signs, you will be more likely to wear your heart on your sleeve, as well as to be more attracted to entertainment, social gatherings and good company. If on the other hand Venus occupied a quiet zodiac sign at the time of your birth, you would tend to be more retiring and less willing to shine in public situations.

It's good to know what part the planet Venus plays in your life, for it can have a great bearing on the way you appear to the rest of the world and since we all have to mix with others, you can learn to make the very best of what Venus has to offer you.

One of the great complications in the past has always been trying to establish exactly what zodiac position Venus enjoyed when you were born, because the planet is notoriously difficult to track. However, I have solved that problem by creating a table that is exclusive to your Sun sign, which you will find on the following page.

Establishing your Venus sign could not be easier. Just look up the year of your birth on the page opposite and you will see a sign of the zodiac. This was the sign that Venus occupied in the period covered by your sign in that year. If Venus occupied more than one sign during the period, this is indicated by the date on which the sign changed, and the name of the new sign. For instance, if you were born in 1950, Venus was in Sagittarius until the 16th December, after which time it was in Capricorn. If you were born before 16th December your Venus sign is Sagittarius, if you were born on or after 16th December, your Venus sign is Capricorn. Once you have established the position of Venus at the time of your birth, you can then look in the pages which follow to see how this has a bearing on your life as a whole.

1918 SAGITTARIUS / 18.12 CAPRICORN
1919 LIBRA / 9.12 SCORPIO
1920 CAPRICORN / 13.12 AQUARIUS
1921 SCORPIO / 7.12 SAGITTARIUS
1922 SAGITTARIUS / 29.11 SCORPIO
1923 SAGITTARIUS / 2.12 CAPRICORN
1924 LIBRA / 27.11 SCORPIO
1925 CAPRICORN / 6.12 AQUARIUS
1926 SAGITTARIUS / 17.12 CAPRICORN
1927 LIBRA / 9.12 SCORPIO
1928 CAPRICORN / 13.12 AQUARIUS
1929 SCORPIO / 7.12 SAGITTARIUS
1930 SCORPIO
1931 SAGITTARIUS / 2.12 CAPRICORN
1932 LIBRA / 26.11 SCORPIO
1933 CAPRICORN / 6.12 AQUARIUS
1934 SAGITTARIUS / 17.12 CAPRICORN
1935 LIBRA / 10.12 SCORPIO
1936 CAPRICORN / 12.12 AQUARIUS
1937 SCORPIO / 6.12 SAGITTARIUS
1938 SCORPIO
1939 SAGITTARIUS / 1.12 CAPRICORN
1940 LIBRA / 26.11 SCORPIO
1941 CAPRICORN / 6.12 AQUARIUS
1942 SAGITTARIUS / 16.12 CAPRICORN
1943 LIBRA / 10.12 SCORPIO
1944 CAPRICORN / 12.12 AQUARIUS
1945 SCORPIO / 6.12 SAGITTARIUS
1946 SCORPIO
1947 SAGITTARIUS / 1.12 CAPRICORN
1948 LIBRA / 25.11 SCORPIO /
    20.12 SAGITTARIUS
1949 CAPRICORN / 7.12 AQUARIUS
1950 SAGITTARIUS / 16.12 CAPRICORN
1951 LIBRA / 10.12 SCORPIO
1952 CAPRICORN / 11.12 AQUARIUS
1953 SCORPIO / 5.12 SAGITTARIUS
1954 SCORPIO
1955 SAGITTARIUS / 30.11 CAPRICORN
1956 LIBRA / 25.11 SCORPIO /
    20.12 SAGITTARIUS
1957 CAPRICORN / 8.12 AQUARIUS
1958 SAGITTARIUS / 15.12 CAPRICORN
1959 LIBRA / 10.12 SCORPIO
1960 CAPRICORN / 11.12 AQUARIUS
1961 SCORPIO / 5.12 SAGITTARIUS
1962 SCORPIO
1963 SAGITTARIUS / 30.11 CAPRICORN
1964 LIBRA / 24.11 SCORPIO /
    19.12 SAGITTARIUS
1965 CAPRICORN / 8.12 AQUARIUS
1966 SAGITTARIUS / 15.12 CAPRICORN
1967 LIBRA / 10.12 SCORPIO

1968 CAPRICORN / 10.12 AQUARIUS
1969 SCORPIO / 4.12 SAGITTARIUS
1970 SCORPIO
1971 SAGITTARIUS / 29.11 CAPRICORN
1972 LIBRA / 24.11 SCORPIO /
    19.12 SAGITTARIUS
1973 CAPRICORN / 9.12 AQUARIUS
1974 SAGITTARIUS / 14.12 CAPRICORN
1975 LIBRA / 9.12 SCORPIO
1976 CAPRICORN / 9.12 AQUARIUS
1977 SCORPIO / 4.12 SAGITTARIUS
1978 SCORPIO
1979 SAGITTARIUS / 28.11 CAPRICORN
1980 SCORPIO / 18.12 SAGITTARIUS
1981 CAPRICORN / 10.12 AQUARIUS
1982 SAGITTARIUS / 14.12 CAPRICORN
1983 LIBRA / 9.12 SCORPIO
1984 CAPRICORN / 9.12 AQUARIUS
1985 SCORPIO / 3.12 SAGITTARIUS
1986 SCORPIO
1987 SAGITTARIUS / 28.11 CAPRICORN
1988 SCORPIO / 18.12 SAGITTARIUS
1989 CAPRICORN / 11.12 AQUARIUS
1990 SAGITTARIUS / 13.12 CAPRICORN
1991 LIBRA / 9.12 SCORPIO
1992 CAPRICORN / 9.12 AQUARIUS
1993 SCORPIO / 3.12 SAGITTARIUS
1994 SCORPIO
1995 SAGITTARIUS / 28.11 CAPRICORN
1996 SCORPIO / 17.12 SAGITTARIUS
1997 CAPRICORN / 12.12 AQUARIUS
1998 SAGITTARIUS / 13.12 CAPRICORN
1999 LIBRA / 9.12 SCORPIO
2000 CAPRICORN / 8.12 AQUARIUS
2001 SCORPIO / 3.12 SAGITTARIUS
2002 SCORPIO
2003 SAGITTARIUS / 28.11 CAPRICORN
2004 SCORPIO / 17.12 SAGITTARIUS
2005 CAPRICORN / 12.12 AQUARIUS
2006 SAGITTARIUS / 13.12 CAPRICORN
2007 LIBRA / 9.12 SCORPIO
2008 CAPRICORN / 8.12 AQUARIUS
2009 SCORPIO / 3.12 AQUARIUS
2010 SCORPIO
2011 SAGITTARIUS / 28.11 CAPRICORN
2012 SCORPIO / 17.12 SAGITTARIUS
2013 SAGITTARIUS / 13.12 CAPRICORN
2014 SAGITTARIUS / 13.12 CAPRICORN
2015 LIBRA / 9.12 SCORPIO
2016 CAPRICORN / 8.12 AQUARIUS

VENUS THROUGH THE ZODIAC SIGNS

Venus in Aries

Amongst other things, the position of Venus in Aries indicates a fondness for travel, music and all creative pursuits. Your nature tends to be affectionate and you would try not to create confusion or difficulty for others if it could be avoided. Many people with this planetary position have a great love of the theatre, and mental stimulation is of the greatest importance. Early romantic attachments are common with Venus in Aries, so it is very important to establish a genuine sense of romantic continuity. Early marriage is not recommended, especially if it is based on sympathy. You may give your heart a little too readily on occasions.

Venus in Taurus

You are capable of very deep feelings and your emotions tend to last for a very long time. This makes you a trusting partner and lover, whose constancy is second to none. In life you are precise and careful and always try to do things the right way. Although this means an ordered life, which you are comfortable with, it can also lead you to be rather too fussy for your own good. Despite your pleasant nature, you are very fixed in your opinions and quite able to speak your mind. Others are attracted to you and historical astrologers always quoted this position of Venus as being very fortunate in terms of marriage. However, if you find yourself involved in a failed relationship, it could take you a long time to trust again.

Venus in Gemini

As with all associations related to Gemini, you tend to be quite versatile, anxious for change and intelligent in your dealings with the world at large. You may gain money from more than one source but you are equally good at spending it. There is an inference here that you are a good communicator, via either the written or the spoken word, and you love to be in the company of interesting people. Always on the look-out for culture, you may also be very fond of music, and love to indulge the curious and cultured side of your nature. In romance you tend to have more than one relationship and could find yourself associated with someone who has previously been a friend or even a distant relative.

Venus in Cancer

You often stay close to home because you are very fond of family and enjoy many of your most treasured moments when you are with those you love. Being naturally sympathetic, you will always do anything you can to support those around you, even people you hardly know at all. This charitable side of your nature is your most noticeable trait and is one of the reasons why others are naturally so fond of you. Being receptive and in some cases even psychic, you can see through to the soul of most of those with whom you come into contact. You may not commence too many romantic attachments but when you do give your heart, it tends to be unconditionally.

Venus in Leo

It must become quickly obvious to almost anyone you meet that you are kind, sympathetic and yet determined enough to stand up for anyone or anything that is truly important to you. Bright and sunny, you warm the world with your natural enthusiasm and would rarely do anything to hurt those around you, or at least not intentionally. In romance you are ardent and sincere, though some may find your style just a little overpowering. Gains come through your contacts with other people and this could be especially true with regard to romance, for love and money often come hand in hand for those who were born with Venus in Leo. People claim to understand you, though you are more complex than you seem.

Venus in Virgo

Your nature could well be fairly quiet no matter what your Sun sign might be, though this fact often manifests itself as an inner peace and would not prevent you from being basically sociable. Some delays and even the odd disappointment in love cannot be ruled out with this planetary position, though it's a fact that you will usually find the happiness you look for in the end. Catapulting yourself into romantic entanglements that you know to be rather ill-advised is not sensible, and it would be better to wait before you committed yourself exclusively to any one person. It is the essence of your nature to serve the world at large and through doing so it is possible that you will attract money at some stage in your life.

Venus in Libra

Venus is very comfortable in Libra and bestows upon those people who have this planetary position a particular sort of kindness that is easy to recognise. This is a very good position for all sorts of friendships and also for romantic attachments that usually bring much joy into your life. Few individuals with Venus in Libra would avoid marriage and since you are capable of great depths of love, it is likely that you will find a contented personal life. You like to mix with people of integrity and intelligence but don't take kindly to scruffy surroundings or work that means getting your hands too dirty. Careful speculation, good business dealings and money through marriage all seem fairly likely.

Venus in Scorpio

You are quite open and tend to spend money quite freely, even on those occasions when you don't have very much. Although your intentions are always good, there are times when you get yourself in to the odd scrape and this can be particularly true when it comes to romance, which you may come to late or from a rather unexpected direction. Certainly you have the power to be happy and to make others contented on the way, but you find the odd stumbling block on your journey through life and it could seem that you have to work harder than those around you. As a result of this, you gain a much deeper understanding of the true value of personal happiness than many people ever do, and are likely to achieve true contentment in the end.

Venus in Sagittarius

You are lighthearted, cheerful and always able to see the funny side of any situation. These facts enhance your popularity, which is especially high with members of the opposite sex. You should never have to look too far to find romantic interest in your life, though it is just possible that you might be too willing to commit yourself before you are certain that the person in question is right for you. Part of the problem here extends to other areas of life too. The fact is that you like variety in everything and so can tire of situations that fail to offer it. All the same, if you choose wisely and learn to understand your restless side, then great happiness can be yours.

Venus in Capricorn

The most notable trait that comes from Venus in this position is that it makes you trustworthy and able to take on all sorts of responsibilities in life. People are instinctively fond of you and love you all the more because you are always ready to help those who are in any form of need. Social and business popularity can be yours and there is a magnetic quality to your nature that is particularly attractive in a romantic sense. Anyone who wants a partner for a lover, a spouse and a good friend too would almost certainly look in your direction. Constancy is the hallmark of your nature and unfaithfulness would go right against the grain. You might sometimes be a little too trusting.

Venus in Aquarius

This location of Venus offers a fondness for travel and a desire to try out something new at every possible opportunity. You are extremely easy to get along with and tend to have many friends from varied backgrounds, classes and inclinations. You like to live a distinct sort of life and gain a great deal from moving about, both in a career sense and with regard to your home. It is not out of the question that you could form a romantic attachment to someone who comes from far away or be attracted to a person of a distinctly artistic and original nature. What you cannot stand is jealousy, for you have friends of both sexes and would want to keep things that way.

Venus in Pisces

The first thing people tend to notice about you is your wonderful, warm smile. Being very charitable by nature you will do anything to help others, even if you don't know them well. Much of your life may be spent sorting out situations for other people, but it is very important to feel that you are living for yourself too. In the main, you remain cheerful, and tend to be quite attractive to members of the opposite sex. Where romantic attachments are concerned, you could be drawn to people who are significantly older or younger than yourself or to someone with a unique career or point of view. It might be best for you to avoid marrying whilst you are still very young.

HOW THE DIAGRAMS WORK

Through the picture diagrams in the Astral Diary I want to help you to plot your year. With them you can see where the positive and negative aspects will be found in each month. To make the most of them, all you have to do is remember where and when!

Let me show you how they work ...

THE MONTH AT A GLANCE

Just as there are twelve separate zodiac signs, so astrologers believe that each sign has twelve separate aspects to life. Each of the twelve segments relates to a different personal aspect. I list them all every month so that their meanings are always clear.

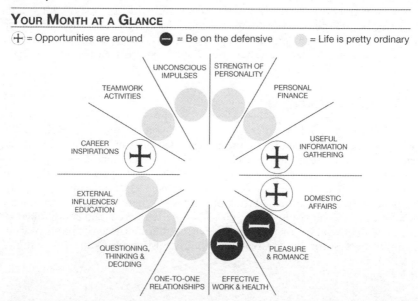

YOUR MONTH AT A GLANCE
⊕ = Opportunities are around   ⊖ = Be on the defensive   ⬤ = Life is pretty ordinary

I have designed this chart to show you how and when these twelve different aspects are being influenced throughout the year. When there is a shaded circle, nothing out of the ordinary is to be expected. However, when a circle turns white with a plus sign, the influence is positive. Where the circle is black with a minus sign, it is a negative.

YOUR ENERGY RHYTHM CHART

Below is a picture diagram in which I link your zodiac group to the rhythm of the Moon. In doing this I have calculated when you will be gaining strength from its influence and equally when you may be weakened by it.

If you think of yourself as being like the tides of the ocean then you may understand how your own energies must also rise and fall. And if you understand how it works and when it is working, then you can better organise your activities to achieve more and get things done more easily.

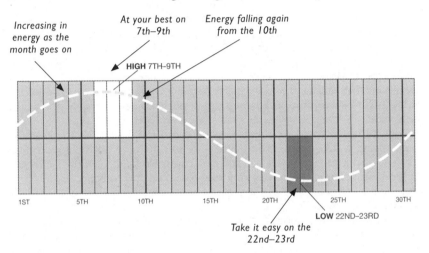

THE KEY DAYS

Some of the entries are in **bold**, which indicates the working of astrological cycles in your life. Look out for them each week as they are the best days to take action or make decisions. The daily text tells you which area of your life to focus on.

MERCURY RETROGRADE

The Mercury symbol (☿) indicates that Mercury is retrograde on that day. Since Mercury governs communication, the fact that it appears to be moving backwards when viewed from the Earth at this time should warn you that your communication skills are not likely to be at their best and you could expect some setbacks.

SAGITTARIUS: YOUR YEAR IN BRIEF

Right at the start of the year you could be called upon to make a great effort of some sort. This is most likely to be associated with work, but wherever it shows your ability to see it through will set the tone for a positive year in 2016. January and February could bring better than average luck and should also be good as far as the social scene is concerned.

The months of March and April bring an ever-greater desire to challenge yourself and to get on well, especially at work. Things should be fairly plain-sailing on the home front but not everyone will behave in quite the way you might expect. Money matters are likely to be stronger and there could be more cash about than you might have expected. Use it as wisely as you can and don't be inclined to splash out on luxuries you don't need and probably don't even really want.

May and June could see things slowing down just a little but the incentive to get ahead is still present. You might have to rely more on the good offices of others at this time, but you will still be anxious to stamp your own authority on most situations. Love comes knocking for some and romance grows along with the first rich blossoms of the year. Be aware that standard responses to old problems may not work.

The warm summer months of July and August are likely to see you at your most active during 2016. Not only is this likely to be a time of travel but you may also be thinking about a change of job, alterations at home and forming new and important friendships. Only your love life seems to be fairly settled during this period but even here young or young-at-heart Archers may well form a new and significant attachment.

During September and October you need to rein in your spending a little, but at the same time you will be feeling fairly comfortable. Both these months could bring new incentives professionally and though far from being the most eventful months of the year they do offer you the possibility of a deeper sense of security and comfort. October, in particular, should offer more in the way of financial gain, most likely as a result of efforts you put in some time ago.

November and December work best for you if you make yourself known. That means rejecting your slight tendency to hold back. When you are at your best you are the hardest worker in the zodiac, and your willingness to get involved at this time will produce great dividends later. A family Christmas is most likely but you could be restless right at the end of the year and may feel the need to ring the changes.

January 2016

YOUR MONTH AT A GLANCE

⊕ = Opportunities are around   ⊖ = Be on the defensive   ⦿ = Life is pretty ordinary

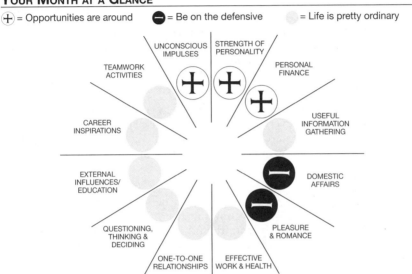

- UNCONSCIOUS IMPULSES
- STRENGTH OF PERSONALITY
- TEAMWORK ACTIVITIES
- PERSONAL FINANCE
- CAREER INSPIRATIONS
- USEFUL INFORMATION GATHERING
- EXTERNAL INFLUENCES/ EDUCATION
- DOMESTIC AFFAIRS
- QUESTIONING, THINKING & DECIDING
- PLEASURE & ROMANCE
- ONE-TO-ONE RELATIONSHIPS
- EFFECTIVE WORK & HEALTH

JANUARY HIGHS AND LOWS

Here I show you how the rhythms of the Moon will affect you this month. Like the tide, your energies and abilities will rise and fall with its pattern. When it is above the centre line, go for it, when it is below, you should be resting.

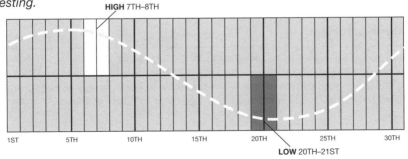

HIGH 7TH–8TH

LOW 20TH–21ST

1ST   5TH   10TH   15TH   20TH   25TH   30TH

45

1 FRIDAY
Moon Age Day 21   Moon Sign Virgo

Your social relationships are generally excellent, although there might be the odd person around today who gives you something of a problem. You get along best with those who cope well with your vibrant and changeable nature and you won't take kindly right now to anyone trying to pull you up in your tracks.

2 SATURDAY
Moon Age Day 22   Moon Sign Libra

Not everything you have to say is going to go down well with everyone you meet today. Although you are very keen to get your ideas across it is just possible that you are rather too brusque in the way you say things at the moment. A large dollop of diplomacy might go a long way.

3 SUNDAY
Moon Age Day 23   Moon Sign Libra

Your attitude is just as friendly and every bit as communicative as usual but you may still not be universally successful because there are some awkward people around who require careful handling. People from the past either come into your mind now or else will be getting in touch with you.

4 MONDAY
Moon Age Day 24   Moon Sign Scorpio

With so many people around making great demands of you, there won't be too much time for personal contemplation. This could turn out to be one of the busiest days of the month and you need to be very organised if you are going to get through everything. Do everything you can to avoid family arguments.

5 TUESDAY
Moon Age Day 25   Moon Sign Scorpio

When it comes to getting your own way the planets are standing in just the right position at the moment. Although you will not be bulldozing your ideas across to others you have a sort of persistence that could easily wear them down. Advancement at work is more likely now than at any other time during January.

6 WEDNESDAY ☿
Moon Age Day 26   Moon Sign Scorpio

You won't take kindly to people who cross you or who show a lack of confidence in your decisions. Avoid acting impetuously and instead listen to what is being said to you. In any case, it is may be better to know the opinion others have of you rather than have this spoken behind your back.

7 THURSDAY ☿ *Moon Age Day 27 Moon Sign Sagittarius*

This should be a great time. The Moon occupies your zodiac sign, bringing that once in a month period known as the lunar high. You are right on the ball and anxious to get on with life in all its varied forms. After so much partying during the festive season it's possible that some people around you may not be so energetic, though.

8 FRIDAY ☿ *Moon Age Day 28 Moon Sign Sagittarius*

You are still very much on the ball and if you are at work today you have what it takes to make the perfect impression on almost everyone. Not only are you very capable at this time you also show your natural charm to an even greater degree. This is the time to impress and to be seen.

9 SATURDAY ☿ *Moon Age Day 0 Moon Sign Capricorn*

You are clearly at your best now when dealing with groups rather than individuals. People tend to look to you for inspiration and will gladly follow your lead under most circumstances. There are also gains to be made on a personal level and a better understanding to be reached with family members.

10 SUNDAY ☿ *Moon Age Day 1 Moon Sign Capricorn*

It is important today to read the small print, no matter what you are doing. That impulsive streak can sometimes get you in a bit of trouble and that's something you need to avoid right now. The fact is that you are sometimes too trusting and fail to appreciate that some individuals are working against your interests.

11 MONDAY ☿ *Moon Age Day 2 Moon Sign Aquarius*

Actions definitely do speak louder than words at the beginning of this new working week. If you want something done it could be better to at least start it yourself. Those around you may be inspired by your enthusiasm and are encouraged by the fact that you are willing to get your own hands dirty.

12 TUESDAY ☿ *Moon Age Day 3 Moon Sign Aquarius*

It might be necessary to show your assertive side today and that could come as something of a surprise to certain people. It doesn't do any harm now and again for you to lay down the law. The problem is that you are often too easy-going for your own good. You can still manage to make people laugh.

13 WEDNESDAY ☿ *Moon Age Day 4 Moon Sign Pisces*

You have some especially innovative ideas around this time and need to be discussing these with others as much as possible. Thinking up a novel way to do something is meat and drink to you and you have what it takes to break tasks down into their component parts.

14 THURSDAY ☿ *Moon Age Day 5 Moon Sign Pisces*

Arguments are not going to get you anywhere, whereas explaining your point of view fully is much more likely to succeed. This is going to test your patience no end because there are people around who refuse to listen, no matter how diplomatic you try to be. It's time to keep your cool.

15 FRIDAY ☿ *Moon Age Day 6 Moon Sign Pisces*

Capitalise on new potential that is turning up all the time. There is plenty to keep you occupied at the moment, both at work and later when you choose to enjoy yourself. A word of warning: it might be advisable to think very carefully about every new strategy, just in case there are too many to deal with all at once.

16 SATURDAY ☿ *Moon Age Day 7 Moon Sign Aries*

There should be strong domestic rewards now for Archers who spend extra time at home. At this time of year you probably won't want to be charging about from pillar to post, although it has to be remembered that present planetary trends may be making you somewhat restless. Try to ring the changes when you can.

17 SUNDAY ☿ *Moon Age Day 8 Moon Sign Aries*

Your social life is now apt to bring significant surprises and finds you doing things you hadn't really planned, probably as a result of the encouragement of friends. With the weekend present you will want to be organising things so that you can have a good time because you are not especially inclined towards work right now.

18 MONDAY ☿ *Moon Age Day 9 Moon Sign Taurus*

The present position of the Sun makes you slightly more restless than of late and you will be quite happy to go with the flow in a social sense, though not if that means standing still for too long. Routines would bore you so try to do something different whenever possible today.

19 TUESDAY ☿ *Moon Age Day 10   Moon Sign Taurus*

This should be a day during which you will be more than happy to stand out in a crowd. Don't be too quick to criticize others, particularly at work, otherwise you may only serve to emphasise your own shortcomings. There are some distinct advantages to being in the right place at the right time now.

20 WEDNESDAY ☿ *Moon Age Day 11   Moon Sign Gemini*

The Moon has now moved into the zodiac sign which is opposite to yours. This brings the monthly period known as the lunar low and is usually a time during which you have to recharge your batteries. It doesn't matter how much effort you put in, things simply don't turn out as you would wish.

21 THURSDAY ☿ *Moon Age Day 12   Moon Sign Gemini*

You might just as well get used to the idea that things are working slowly because for all the effort you expound there is likely to be little gain today. Instead, use this time to plan ahead and clear the decks for action later. Catch up on conversations with family members and a good friend.

22 FRIDAY ☿ *Moon Age Day 13   Moon Sign Cancer*

It looks as though you will need to be just a little more careful with money at present, mainly because there may be amounts to spend that you had not expected. You can make more money in the longer-term but for the moment you will probably have to keep your purse or wallet closed to new purchases.

23 SATURDAY ☿ *Moon Age Day 14   Moon Sign Cancer*

It might be somewhat difficult to make decisions today, almost certainly because there is more than one option and they all look particularly good. The attitude of a friend or a family member could be somewhat difficult to understand and you need to be just a little careful not to give unintentional offence.

24 SUNDAY ☿ *Moon Age Day 15   Moon Sign Leo*

You need to remain assertive and to let the world know exactly what you want from it. Don't be vague in any situation and turn your attention to those matters that you know to be the most important in a practical and a financial sense. Personal relationships may not receive too much attention now.

25 MONDAY ☿

Moon Age Day 16   Moon Sign Leo

There is great optimism about now and a sense that things are going your way. Although you may be slightly hampered in your efforts to get ahead financially, that isn't really what today is all about. Rather you will be making headway in all attachments, both personal ones and simple friendships.

26 TUESDAY ☿

Moon Age Day 17   Moon Sign Leo

A hectic period and a time during which you will have to work hard in order to keep up with all that is expected of you. Someone you don't see often may return to your life and bring with them a breath of fresh air. As usual you will be keen to persuade everyone around you to see your strong points.

27 WEDNESDAY

Moon Age Day 18   Moon Sign Virgo

Although today may be enjoyable, you could find that there are changes in the offing at work that you don't like the look of. Before you raise direct objections it would be sensible to think things through very carefully. By the end of the day you will have your mind set on socialising.

28 THURSDAY

Moon Age Day 19   Moon Sign Virgo

You appear to be thinking about personal goals and objectives at the moment and will be quite happy to let the responsibilities of your life take something of a holiday. This would be a good day for a shopping spree or for thinking about some very early but quite necessary spring-cleaning.

29 FRIDAY

Moon Age Day 20   Moon Sign Libra

The end of the working week for many of you brings a day during which some frustrations will exist. You probably will not be able to get others round to your way of thinking. This can be particularly difficult when you are certain in your own mind that your beliefs are absolutely true.

30 SATURDAY

Moon Age Day 21   Moon Sign Libra

Look for a little nostalgia at the moment but don't live in the past. The Archer is generally committed to the future rather than times that are gone and you can get a little down in the dumps if you dwell on things too much. The attitude of friends is good and they will be doing all they can to make you happy.

31 SUNDAY

Moon Age Day 22   Moon Sign Libra

This is definitely a good time during which to take a centre-stage position. The fact is that you are snappy, good to know and very, very exciting to have around. If there are people who don't quite realise what you are worth, leave them alone and concentrate on those who have no difficulty seeing your magic.

February 2016

YOUR MONTH AT A GLANCE

⊕ = Opportunities are around   ⊖ = Be on the defensive   ⬤ = Life is pretty ordinary

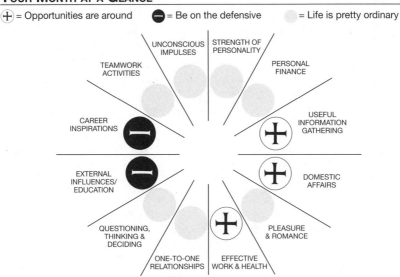

UNCONSCIOUS IMPULSES

STRENGTH OF PERSONALITY

TEAMWORK ACTIVITIES

PERSONAL FINANCE

CAREER INSPIRATIONS

USEFUL INFORMATION GATHERING

EXTERNAL INFLUENCES/ EDUCATION

DOMESTIC AFFAIRS

QUESTIONING, THINKING & DECIDING

PLEASURE & ROMANCE

ONE-TO-ONE RELATIONSHIPS

EFFECTIVE WORK & HEALTH

FEBRUARY HIGHS AND LOWS

Here I show you how the rhythms of the Moon will affect you this month. Like the tide, your energies and abilities will rise and fall with its pattern. When it is above the centre line, go for it, when it is below, you should be resting.

HIGH 3RD–5TH

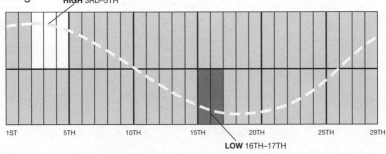

1ST   5TH   10TH   15TH   20TH   25TH   29TH

LOW 16TH–17TH

52

1 MONDAY
Moon Age Day 23   Moon Sign Scorpio

Those in a position of authority over you are now likely to be taking notice of your abilities so it's worth being on the ball today. Friends should prove to be quite supportive at the moment and one or two of them might be anxious to repay a favour they had from you some time ago.

2 TUESDAY
Moon Age Day 24   Moon Sign Scorpio

Although you are likely to be quite busy you should not overlook social matters – these are also important. Family members and friends alike give you reason to be proud for much of this week and someone is likely to especially successful, partly as a result of the assistance you have given.

3 WEDNESDAY
Moon Age Day 25   Moon Sign Sagittarius

The Moon sails into your zodiac sign and the resulting lunar high finds you in the most confident of moods and anxious to get ahead in a dozen different ways. Only the Archer could keep so many balls in the air at the same time and this is a day during which you may surprise yourself and everyone else too.

4 THURSDAY
Moon Age Day 26   Moon Sign Sagittarius

The positive trends continue and there isn't much point in waiting around for the rest of the world to catch up in a practical sense. You know what you want from life and have a pretty good idea how to get it. Social trends are the best of all so look for ways in which to bring people out of their shells today.

5 FRIDAY
Moon Age Day 27   Moon Sign Sagittarius

Co-operation is the key to success and this applies just as much to social and romantic possibilities as it does to your work. There's no doubt that today you should end up being the leader of the pack but your ability to delegate remains important – if only because you can't do everything yourself.

6 SATURDAY
Moon Age Day 28   Moon Sign Capricorn

Your confidence remains generally high, even if you do not always feel yourself capable of achieving what others expect. Stretching yourself is important because it can teach you things about your own nature that you never suspected. Be prepared for social arrangements to be changed at short notice.

7 SUNDAY
Moon Age Day 29   Moon Sign Capricorn

If you are not entirely sure what direction your personal life is taking, the best course of action is to simply wait and see. Not everyone is behaving quite as you might expect and as a result you will have to be very flexible. Responding to situations at short-notice is not at all difficult for the Archer.

8 MONDAY
Moon Age Day 0   Moon Sign Aquarius

The more you seek out the company of people you genuinely like, the greater are the potential successes of today. Most of these will be social in nature because trends suggest that you may not be focused on professional progress for a day or two. Family members could prove to be both intriguing and slightly frustrating.

9 TUESDAY
Moon Age Day 1   Moon Sign Aquarius

What sets today apart is not your gains at work but rather what you achieve once the responsibilities of the day are out of the way. For real success you need to be able to mix business with pleasure. You might also make an ally who could be of tremendous use to you in the weeks and months to come.

10 WEDNESDAY
Moon Age Day 2   Moon Sign Pisces

Today could be quite lucky and the real assistance on offer comes by virtue of the position of the Moon in your solar chart right now. Your emotional responses are good and you come across positively in personal situations. Keep in touch with old workmates and people you once saw on a regular basis.

11 THURSDAY
Moon Age Day 3   Moon Sign Pisces

There are many new ideas around at this time and picking out the best of them is something you don't find at all difficult. Rehearse what you want to say in professional situations but don't be in the least surprised if what actually comes out of your mouth is very different indeed.

12 FRIDAY
Moon Age Day 4   Moon Sign Aries

Great things can happen today if you are willing to express your innermost feelings and if you respond positively to the things others have to say. Romance is especially well-starred and Sagittarians who have been looking for a new love would be well advised to concentrate their efforts around this time.

13 SATURDAY   *Moon Age Day 5   Moon Sign Aries*

Hard work pays dividends and you make significant progress at least partly because of your natural ingenuity. Acting on impulse is something that is instinctive to you and your spontaneous attitude is certainly infectious. Ignore the negative trends brought about by people who are pessimistic.

14 SUNDAY   *Moon Age Day 6   Moon Sign Taurus*

Today could be slightly quieter than yesterday, but it still offers good opportunities for some advancement. You take the time to look at situations carefully and will be quite contemplative on occasions. There is more planning today than action but in the longer-term this may turn out to be a very good thing.

15 MONDAY   *Moon Age Day 7   Moon Sign Taurus*

In terms of your professional aspirations the planets are shining on you now. It will be worth putting in that extra bit of effort to demonstrate how capable you are. If it means working a few more hours you should do so, because the possible rewards are significant. Romance may take a backseat at the start of this week.

16 TUESDAY   *Moon Age Day 8   Moon Sign Gemini*

You are greatly appreciated by most of the people you come across at the moment, which is just as well because you will probably have to call upon their assistance whilst the lunar low is around. You simply are not working at your best today and could do with a few hours to yourself at some stage.

17 WEDNESDAY   *Moon Age Day 9   Moon Sign Gemini*

You could still find yourself facing some uphill challenges and won't have what it takes to sort everything out for yourself. Rely on the support that comes from those you trust the most, though it is also likely that you will have to rely on strangers more than you might actually wish to do.

18 THURSDAY   *Moon Age Day 10   Moon Sign Cancer*

You should be feeling fairly ambitious today and will want to get on quickly with anything that is on your mind. The only problem is that your friends and colleagues may not feel quite the same way. However, even if you have to go it alone you should find yourself succeeding most of the time.

19 FRIDAY

Moon Age Day 11   Moon Sign Cancer

You remain generally happy with your lot but you may have to modify your ideas at short-notice for maximum benefit. This is not at all hard for the Archer and you prove yourself to be as adaptable as ever. Keep in touch with valued friends, especially those who are far from home at present.

20 SATURDAY

Moon Age Day 12   Moon Sign Cancer

Realising how important first impressions can be, you now spend a good deal of your time bringing people round to your specific point of view. This is achieved with a combination of flattery and gentle bullying. You see this as being essential, not only for your sake but for theirs too.

21 SUNDAY

Moon Age Day 13   Moon Sign Leo

Progress remains generally good but this being a Sunday you probably should not expect to be getting too much done. In any case it would be good to spend some time with your partner or family members and too much go-getting could easily get in the way of simple enjoyment.

22 MONDAY

Moon Age Day 14   Moon Sign Leo

You can probably get further with your career ambitions now than at any other time during February. You clearly know what you want and have a very good idea how to load any dice in your favour. Don't expect the whole world to be on your side but the people who matter the most will be.

23 TUESDAY

Moon Age Day 15   Moon Sign Virgo

For those Sagittarians who have been slightly off colour during the last couple of days, things are now likely to be looking better. Don't be too worried if loved ones seem a touch out of sorts but pay them the attention they deserve and be there for them if they feel they want to talk.

24 WEDNESDAY

Moon Age Day 16   Moon Sign Virgo

It is towards friendship and social activities that you tend to turn at the moment and you should find romance to be especially rewarding. The Archer is now taking time out to look closely at specific issues and this means you are less likely to make mistakes and should see small successes coming along.

25 THURSDAY
Moon Age Day 17   Moon Sign Libra

Trends suggest that you will enjoy some pleasant activities now, most likely in the company of those you count as good friends. At the same time you are extremely communicative and could be responsible for dozens of text messages, emails or letters. Important news may come in from family members.

26 FRIDAY
Moon Age Day 18   Moon Sign Libra

Sagittarius may be inclined to be just a little selfish at the moment and it would be sensible to analyse your motivations in every situation before you proceed with it. What you don't need right now is to make an enemy, especially as it isn't necessary to do so. Balance your dynamic attitude with a tendency towards diplomacy.

27 SATURDAY
Moon Age Day 19   Moon Sign Libra

You will meet people around now who are going to have a big part to play in your longer-term future. All the planetary trends show that this is a good time to make new friends and you have a strong influence on the way others think. When approaching anything new, attitude is all-important.

28 SUNDAY
Moon Age Day 20   Moon Sign Scorpio

Some of your present aims and objectives may be slightly unrealistic and it might be sensible to look at a few of them again, this time paying proper attention to them. Outside of practicalities you could be adopting new interests and some of these are likely to have a distinctly intellectual quality.

29 MONDAY
Moon Age Day 21   Moon Sign Scorpio

A slightly quieter spell overtakes you as the Moon passes through your solar twelfth house. You may be feeling contemplative and apt to look at situations carefully, taking your time over decisions to ensure that things turn out right. Don't be too quick to form a judgement regarding a particular family issue.

March

2016

YOUR MONTH AT A GLANCE

(+) = Opportunities are around   (−) = Be on the defensive   ● = Life is pretty ordinary

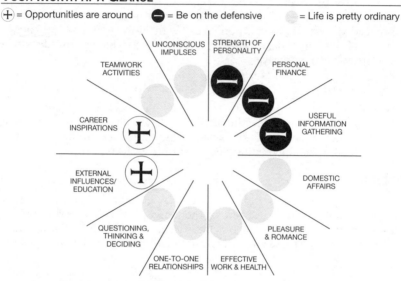

STRENGTH OF PERSONALITY

UNCONSCIOUS IMPULSES

TEAMWORK ACTIVITIES

PERSONAL FINANCE

CAREER INSPIRATIONS

USEFUL INFORMATION GATHERING

EXTERNAL INFLUENCES/ EDUCATION

DOMESTIC AFFAIRS

QUESTIONING, THINKING & DECIDING

PLEASURE & ROMANCE

ONE-TO-ONE RELATIONSHIPS

EFFECTIVE WORK & HEALTH

MARCH HIGHS AND LOWS

Here I show you how the rhythms of the Moon will affect you this month. Like the tide, your energies and abilities will rise and fall with its pattern. When it is above the centre line, go for it, when it is below, you should be resting.

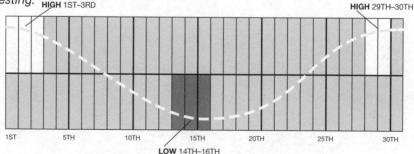

HIGH 1ST–3RD

HIGH 29TH–30TH

1ST   5TH   10TH   15TH   20TH   25TH   30TH

LOW 14TH–16TH

1 TUESDAY
Moon Age Day 22   Moon Sign Sagittarius

In sudden and quite dramatic style the lunar high finds you raring to go and back to being the sort of person most people have come to expect. With plenty of vitality, great optimism and a determination to get on top of all the issues in your life, you have what it takes to make a real splash.

2 WEDNESDAY
Moon Age Day 23   Moon Sign Sagittarius

Another good day comes along and one during which Lady Luck is likely to be on your side. You can afford to take a few chances and enjoy pushing the bounds of the possible. The Archer is usually an adventurous soul and this certainly seems to be the case at the end of this quite surprising period.

3 THURSDAY
Moon Age Day 24   Moon Sign Sagittarius

Keep on the right side of people who are in a good position to put your name forward for something important. You won't do yourself any favours by falling out with those who can have a bearing on your future. The Archer can be a little touchy right now but these are trends that can be modified with self-control.

4 FRIDAY
Moon Age Day 25   Moon Sign Capricorn

When it comes to the deepest issues in life you show a great and an instinctive understanding. Superficial concerns won't be your thing at the moment and it's clear that Sagittarius is in the mood to probe. On the way you should be in a good position to help someone whose own problems go back a long way.

5 SATURDAY
Moon Age Day 26   Moon Sign Capricorn

You show great concern for others and will be doing all you can to be both loving and supportive. All the attention you give to others ensures that your personal popularity remains high and it's possible that the one who ends up winning out the most is you. Your mind is very analytical around this time.

6 SUNDAY
Moon Age Day 27   Moon Sign Aquarius

Avoid conflicts with others if you know that there is nothing positive to be gained from them. It is not likely to be you who is tetchy and inclined to fly off the handle but it takes two people to make a dispute and if you refuse to be involved things will soon settle down. Instead, get on with something practical.

7 MONDAY
Moon Age Day 28   Moon Sign Aquarius

Take some time out for family discussions and make sure that you explain yourself more fully than you might have done in the recent past. Family outings could be fun, or some time spent with friends you don't see too often. If congratulations are in order somewhere in the family, lay them on with a trowel.

8 TUESDAY
Moon Age Day 0   Moon Sign Pisces

Your sensitive side is once again on display and much of what you do today is undertaken for the sake of people who are dear to you. Achieving your own objectives won't be hard but the real gains are of a personal nature. This is likely to be an important time for sending and receiving letters, emails or text messages.

9 WEDNESDAY
Moon Age Day 1   Moon Sign Pisces

Your judgement tends to be sound at present and you will rarely put a foot wrong. The problem is that when you do make a mistake it's likely to be a major one. The only person who is going to be left red in the face is you and so a little forethought can go a long way at the moment.

10 THURSDAY
Moon Age Day 2   Moon Sign Aries

Sit back and watch life for a few hours today and maybe spend some time out of doors so that you can register just how much is changing with the advance of the spring. There will be very little to tempt you into dynamic action today, so you may as well enjoy the enforced break from your usual Sagittarian ways.

11 FRIDAY
Moon Age Day 3   Moon Sign Aries

Don't overspend at present. There is a tendency for your enthusiasm to run away with you and although you probably deserve a little luxury, it might be best to wait before you part with your hard-earned cash. Better bargains should be on offer before long and in any case money could be somewhat tight right now.

12 SATURDAY
Moon Age Day 4   Moon Sign Taurus

Don't allow your ego to get in the way when it comes to making sensible decisions. In almost any situation you know what you should do and your practical common sense should be your guide at present. There is a strong possibility that a new romantic proposal will be on the way for quite a few Sagittarians around now.

13 SUNDAY *Moon Age Day 5   Moon Sign Taurus*

Although you need to be quite realistic at this time it's also very important to push the bounds of the possible. Achieving this balance won't be easy but remains essential if you want to get on well. In all practical situations you tend to be assertive, probably to the slight frustration of your friends.

14 MONDAY *Moon Age Day 6   Moon Sign Gemini*

Although you want to get things done, chances are that you just don't have the energy. It's as if you have run out of steam for the moment but this is a situation that will reverse itself very quickly. Stick to people you know and to situations that don't tax you any more than necessary.

15 TUESDAY *Moon Age Day 7   Moon Sign Gemini*

Trends are still quiet, mainly because the monthly lunar low is around. It won't do you any harm at all to stand and watch life go by for a while. At the same time you are in the right mood to finally address issues that might have been on your mind for a while now, so pay these some long-overdue attention.

16 WEDNESDAY *Moon Age Day 8   Moon Sign Gemini*

This should be a rather good day from a personal point of view with plenty to keep you occupied and some new social input coming along. Relationships are likely to work especially well for you and there should be plenty of interactions with people who are in a position to offer you some assistance.

17 THURSDAY *Moon Age Day 9   Moon Sign Cancer*

You show a great interest in the world at large and will be more than happy to get yourself involved in new activities of one sort or another. Your capacity to mix business with pleasure has hardly ever been better and you find yourself happy to sort out some sort of mess created by a loved one.

18 FRIDAY *Moon Age Day 10   Moon Sign Cancer*

If you get the chance to push beyond the normal boundaries and do something completely different today you should grab the opportunity with both hands. Getting down to some hard work might not be very appealing but you will be glad you applied yourself when the benefits start to come in.

19 SATURDAY
Moon Age Day 11   Moon Sign Leo

If things are not going fast enough for you right now, you do have what it takes to speed life up. This takes extra effort, however, and it is true that there is a slightly lazy streak about you at present. The ideal situation is to make gains as a result of the actions of others, whilst you watch on and applaud!

20 SUNDAY
Moon Age Day 12   Moon Sign Leo

You can't expect to be on the ball through every moment of the day on this Sunday but if you restrict yourself to one activity at a time, everything should work out reasonably well. You won't be exactly firing on all cylinders but if you bluff your way through the day that won't matter either.

21 MONDAY
Moon Age Day 13   Moon Sign Virgo

If there are any decisions to be made, you could hardly choose a better day than this. Your reasoning is sound and you will have sufficient time to think about things. Having to alter your social diary might be something of a bore but what comes along for today should be interesting enough, even if it is unexpected.

22 TUESDAY
Moon Age Day 14   Moon Sign Virgo

You need to be much more selective, especially about someone you call a close friend. Not everyone is worthy of the name, though the people you have known for a long time should come good under all circumstances. Keep your eyes open because deception is possible under present planetary trends.

23 WEDNESDAY
Moon Age Day 15   Moon Sign Virgo

Take time out to look more carefully at your personal life. The trouble is that you get so busy you don't always pay as much attention as you should to the person with whom you share your life. Make a special fuss of them today and even if there is no anniversary to celebrate you could invent one.

24 THURSDAY
Moon Age Day 16   Moon Sign Libra

There is hardly anything today that will faze you and you take great delight in doing things for the first time. Not everyone is equally confident and you may have to offer a good deal of support from time to time. This will be especially true in the case of timorous colleagues or younger family members.

25 FRIDAY
Moon Age Day 17   Moon Sign Libra

Though you want to do all you can to help people today, it won't always be possible. You need to look at your own life too, and to do all you can to get things straight for a big push that is just around the corner. Spending time with loved ones in the evening might be both appealing and rewarding.

26 SATURDAY
Moon Age Day 18   Moon Sign Scorpio

There is a great deal of optimism about at the present time and a special desire to commit yourself to new and interesting strategies. The Archer is coming into its own in all sorts of ways and there are exciting new opportunities around every corner. Give some help to a friend who is rather depressed.

27 SUNDAY
Moon Age Day 19   Moon Sign Scorpio

If you get the chance to travel you need to grab the chance with both hands. There are some interesting diversions in the offing and new people to meet. What probably pleases you the most at present is being able to help out those who have got themselves into something of a muddle.

28 MONDAY
Moon Age Day 20   Moon Sign Scorpio

Settle for something quiet and relaxing if that is at all possible today. Don't get bogged down with boring jobs and if they simply have to be done, get them out of the way early in the day. Trends suggest that people you don't see very often could be getting in touch, or even turning up unexpectedly.

29 TUESDAY
Moon Age Day 21   Moon Sign Sagittarius

Apply yourself fully from the moment you rise this morning and take advantage of the very real possibilities that this day contains. You may be acting almost entirely on impulse but you are so insightful that you can make all manner of gains without really trying. Most important of all, your popularity is high.

30 WEDNESDAY
Moon Age Day 22   Moon Sign Sagittarius

The lunar high offers new incentives and it is abundantly clear that you will be anxious to try something different, especially in a social sense. You may also be getting yourself ready for what could be a busy week that lies ahead and a little prior planning now will pay dividends later.

31 THURSDAY
Moon Age Day 23   Moon Sign Capricorn

Promises made to you at this time may prove to be less than reliable so it's worth checking all details for yourself. In the end you might decide that it would simply be easier to undertake most tasks yourself in the first place. You are quite artistic at the moment and need to find new outlets for your creativity.

April

2016

Your Month at a Glance

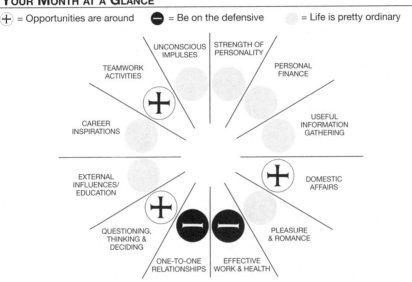

April Highs and Lows

Here I show you how the rhythms of the Moon will affect you this month. Like the tide, your energies and abilities will rise and fall with its pattern. When it is above the centre line, go for it, when it is below, you should be resting.

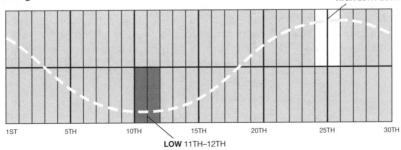

1 FRIDAY
Moon Age Day 24   Moon Sign Capricorn

Avoid spending too much at the moment because you might find that you regret it later. When it comes to really enjoying your life the things that appeal the most won't cost you a penny. Friendship is especially important around now and you will probably be including new people in your life.

2 SATURDAY
Moon Age Day 25   Moon Sign Capricorn

The planets suggest that there is a good day in store for Sagittarius today. It's the little things that others do for you that are touching and you are likely to be pushing the bounds of the credible in at least some ways. Get away from routines when you can and if possible start the weekend by doing something different.

3 SUNDAY
Moon Age Day 26   Moon Sign Aquarius

What you probably relish more than anything right now is being in the company of particularly interesting people. The way you respond to the world at large is typical of your Sagittarian heritage, so getting on with just about anyone is a piece of cake. Adaptable is your middle name at present.

4 MONDAY
Moon Age Day 27   Moon Sign Aquarius

Attracting money won't be hard, but neither will be spending it. Cash seems to slip through your fingers like water around now and you need to make conscious and sometimes hard-fought decisions to save a little. Friends should prove inspirational in some way and you need to show them your gratitude.

5 TUESDAY
Moon Age Day 28   Moon Sign Pisces

You need to stop yourself from swelling up with pride just because something goes right. There is great truth in the adage that pride goes before a fall and there are certainly stumbles along the way if you are not careful right now. Listen carefully to the sound advice of someone older or wiser.

6 WEDNESDAY
Moon Age Day 29   Moon Sign Pisces

If you feel that you lack some direction today, spend time looking around and thinking through situations as carefully as you can. There is no need to feel in any way isolated because wherever your mind is going at the moment, someone close to you has been there before and can offer a guiding hand.

7 THURSDAY
Moon Age Day 0   Moon Sign Aries

This might be as good a time as any to take a close look at your personal finances and to try to whip them into shape. Details don't interest you as a rule because it's the broad spectrum of life that attracts your attention. However, you have the ability to concentrate under present planetary trends and would be well advised to exploit this.

8 FRIDAY
Moon Age Day 1   Moon Sign Aries

Once again it appears that you are focusing your attention on money – or more likely how to acquire more of it. You have great ingenuity but what would really help is to make up your mind to a particular course of action and then to stick to it. Getting help when you need it should be child's play today.

9 SATURDAY
Moon Age Day 2   Moon Sign Taurus

Tricky situations that would bamboozle others won't bother you in the least. You love a challenge and relish the prospect of having to think on your feet. Today should prove to be inspiring and fascinating. Intellectual stimulation comes from a number of different directions and new people enter your life.

10 SUNDAY
Moon Age Day 3   Moon Sign Taurus

The pressure is on and you may feel there is something very important to prove. Whether or not this turns out to be the case doesn't really matter because it's your frame of mind that rules the roost now. Remember that when you are involved in work situations around this time, actions speak louder than words.

11 MONDAY
Moon Age Day 4   Moon Sign Gemini

This is a Monday during which you are likely to be quite mellow and contemplative. The lunar low won't really bother you unless you insist on trying to push ahead in some sphere of your life. Keep your wishes moderate and spend time with people who make you feel happy just to be alive.

12 TUESDAY
Moon Age Day 5   Moon Sign Gemini

You may decide that this would be the right time for advancement at work but there could be delays and you may have to wait for a while. This part of the week certainly won't be as positive as you would wish – another legacy of the lunar low. By tomorrow, though, you should be right back on form.

13 WEDNESDAY
Moon Age Day 6   Moon Sign Cancer

A bright and breezy attitude, allied to a very keen sense of humour, is a key component in the way you approach the world today. People should be glad to have you around and do all they can to encourage you. Don't take offence when criticism comes along because it's likely to be constructive.

14 THURSDAY
Moon Age Day 7   Moon Sign Cancer

Any sort of progress looks possible today and the only slightly difficult situation lies in knowing which area of your life to focus on. In the end, in line with your usual Sagittarian nature, you may decide to cherry-pick. You do possess a good ability to mix business with pleasure at this time.

15 FRIDAY
Moon Age Day 8   Moon Sign Leo

Distractions are nothing new for Sagittarius because they crop up all the time. You probably don't understand the meaning of the word boredom and certainly won't be short of something interesting to do. All the same, a temporary quieter interlude could descend before this day comes to its close.

16 SATURDAY
Moon Age Day 9   Moon Sign Leo

You can help yourself greatly now by doing something that isn't strictly necessary but which you know will make the future easier for all concerned. Romance seems to be knocking at your door all the time during the coming days and you have what it takes to turn heads in a social as well as a personal sense.

17 SUNDAY
Moon Age Day 10   Moon Sign Virgo

Family matters tend to be very rewarding now and you are likely to spend as much time as you can with loved ones. Keep confidences because people are relying on you and won't take kindly to you spreading their business far and wide. Most important of all you need to be careful in whom you confide.

18 MONDAY
Moon Age Day 11   Moon Sign Virgo

Keep your purse or wallet firmly closed today unless you are certain of a bargain. The fact is that you are likely to be duped at the moment and there is nothing you can do about this except to exercise extreme caution. This would not be a good day to sign documents unless you have read the small print very carefully.

19 TUESDAY
Moon Age Day 12   Moon Sign Virgo

It is towards the practical aspects of life that you are apt to turn today. You want to get things done and the only way you know is to get stuck in. You may want everything your own way, regardless of the wishes of others. There is a tendency for the Archer to be a little unreasonable now, so try to rein this in.

20 WEDNESDAY
Moon Age Day 13   Moon Sign Libra

There are times today when you can prove to be positively inspirational but at the same time there are obstacles being placed in your path. Start early in the day with practical jobs and that way you will have a few hours later to please yourself. If possible find time for a breath of fresh air.

21 THURSDAY
Moon Age Day 14   Moon Sign Libra

This could prove to be one of the most assertive days of the month as far as you are concerned. It might be difficult getting others motivated and that is one of your tests for today. Colleagues in particular may seem unwilling to commit themselves, so be prepared for some gentle shoving to be necessary.

22 FRIDAY
Moon Age Day 15   Moon Sign Libra

It is towards the intimate side of your life that your mind keeps turning now. You want to find some way to show your partner or sweetheart just how important they are to you and as a result you will be turning your originality up to full. Not all those around you respond to your charm – but you can't please everyone.

23 SATURDAY   ☿
Moon Age Day 16   Moon Sign Scorpio

You want to do everything you can to maximise your potential at the moment and the weekend is no obstacle to your forward progress in life. You should be feeling good about yourself and able to move forward on a number of fronts. Finances are likely to look stronger, but beware that this may be something of an illusion.

24 SUNDAY   ☿
Moon Age Day 17   Moon Sign Scorpio

You have a very practical turn of mind today and want to get things done, especially at work. There ought to be plenty of co-operation about and it looks as though you will be getting on very well when in group situations. Don't be surprised if others insist that you take the lead.

25 MONDAY ☿ *Moon Age Day 18 Moon Sign Sagittarius*

Things now go pretty much the way you would wish and although you are going to be very busy, the next couple of days should prove to be both fascinating and illuminating. Even the little things of life bring their own joy whilst the lunar high is around and you will be both active and enterprising.

26 TUESDAY ☿ *Moon Age Day 19 Moon Sign Sagittarius*

With no lack of energy and a helping hand from a number of different directions, it is now possible to make the sort of progress that might have eluded you earlier in the month. It's time to concentrate your efforts and to make one serious push in a favoured direction. Self-belief is certainly the key now.

27 WEDNESDAY ☿ *Moon Age Day 20 Moon Sign Capricorn*

Although some caution is indicated today this is probably not going to prevent you from taking chances. Sagittarius sometimes rushes in where angels fear to tread but you usually get away with it. Your powers of communication are good and you have the look of someone who could persuade anyone around to their way of thinking.

28 THURSDAY ☿ *Moon Age Day 21 Moon Sign Capricorn*

There isn't much doubt about your optimism at present but you might have to curb it now and again in favour of practical and sound judgements. Of course you want to show everyone how capable you are but unless you exercise just a little care and caution you could come unstuck in a particularly embarrassing way.

29 FRIDAY ☿ *Moon Age Day 22 Moon Sign Capricorn*

It's true that there are challenges about but these only add to your desire to get ahead in a general sense. You need change and diversity all the time around now and should ring the changes as far as your social life is concerned. Keep in touch with family members and maybe arrange a reunion of some sort.

30 SATURDAY ☿ *Moon Age Day 23 Moon Sign Aquarius*

It seems that you will be led by your curiosity at the end of this month, and the realisation that the warm weather is now on the way brings you great happiness. This makes you want to spread your wings and even if you can't go anywhere today, you can at least dream and plan.

May

2016

Your Month at a Glance

(+) = Opportunities are around   ● = Be on the defensive   ○ = Life is pretty ordinary

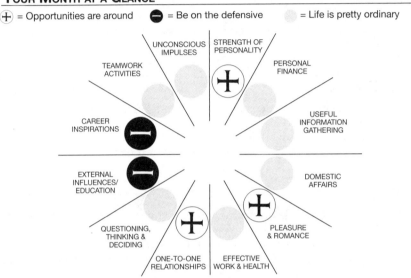

UNCONSCIOUS IMPULSES

STRENGTH OF PERSONALITY

TEAMWORK ACTIVITIES

PERSONAL FINANCE

CAREER INSPIRATIONS

USEFUL INFORMATION GATHERING

EXTERNAL INFLUENCES/ EDUCATION

DOMESTIC AFFAIRS

QUESTIONING, THINKING & DECIDING

PLEASURE & ROMANCE

ONE-TO-ONE RELATIONSHIPS

EFFECTIVE WORK & HEALTH

May Highs and Lows

Here I show you how the rhythms of the Moon will affect you this month. Like the tide, your energies and abilities will rise and fall with its pattern. When it is above the centre line, go for it, when it is below, you should be resting.

HIGH 22ND–24TH

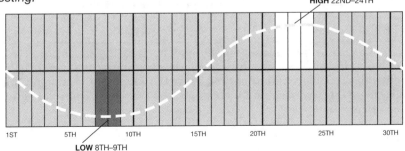

1ST   5TH   10TH   15TH   20TH   25TH   30TH

LOW 8TH–9TH

1 SUNDAY ☿ *Moon Age Day 24   Moon Sign Aquarius*

The way you view the world today has a lot to do with how you are going to get on in a general sense. It is most likely that your Sagittarian enthusiasm and optimism are shining out like beacons to such an extent that others could hardly fail to notice. As a result you will receive plenty of attention.

2 MONDAY ☿ *Moon Age Day 25   Moon Sign Pisces*

Although you will now be slightly more contemplative, this ought to be the sort of day during which you show your efficiency. You won't need too much in order to get ahead and you tend to be generally economical. This is just as well because planetary trends pointing towards greater wealth are thin on the ground.

3 TUESDAY ☿ *Moon Age Day 26   Moon Sign Pisces*

Not everyone seems to understand you around this time and you will have to work hard in order to explain yourself. This probably isn't your fault but it won't do you any harm at all to stretch your intellect a little. The creative side of the Archer is likely to be on display both today and for several days to come.

4 WEDNESDAY ☿ *Moon Age Day 27   Moon Sign Aries*

Don't hold back today. If you feel something you should speak out. A slight word of warning would be that you may not be at your most diplomatic so you will have to work hard if you want to avoid standing on the toes of other people. Social trends look good and you respond well to changes in midweek routines.

5 THURSDAY ☿ *Moon Age Day 28   Moon Sign Aries*

Having to take on additional responsibilities could leave you feeling somewhat thwarted today and you would be well advised to spread the load a little by enlisting the support of those with whom you come into contact. You should find colleagues and friends more than willing to lend a hand.

6 FRIDAY ☿ *Moon Age Day 0   Moon Sign Taurus*

Keep in touch with people, no matter how far away they might be. This is no time to hide in your own little shell, despite the fact that you may feel slightly threatened from time to time. Have the courage of your convictions and when you have made up your mind to a particular course of action, keep going.

7 SATURDAY ☿   *Moon Age Day 1   Moon Sign Taurus*

It looks as though romance is the best area of life to pursue this Saturday. At the same time all social trends look particularly good, so take the day to do whatever you like, if you can. It is likely that you will choose something that is purely for fun. You also enjoy a great ability to support relatives and friends.

8 SUNDAY ☿   *Moon Age Day 2   Moon Sign Gemini*

Stand by for a very quiet spell at this stage of the month and don't expect too much of either yourself or those around you. It would be better to do one job properly at the moment rather than to undertake half a dozen and get none of them right. This is also a good period during which you can think ahead.

9 MONDAY ☿   *Moon Age Day 3   Moon Sign Gemini*

Starting anything new at the moment is not to be recommended. Rather you need to sit quietly and to think about what you might do tomorrow. Rules and regulations have a tendency to get on your nerves and all you really want to do is to spend time on your own, maybe reading or catching up on letters and emails.

10 TUESDAY ☿   *Moon Age Day 4   Moon Sign Cancer*

Everyday life should become more informative and interesting as the week progresses. Find something different to do today and don't be held back by the adverse reactions of a single person. Some people were just born to be pessimists but that's not your way at all. Remain convinced of your own abilities.

11 WEDNESDAY ☿   *Moon Age Day 5   Moon Sign Cancer*

This is likely to be a good time for attacking problems and for coming to terms with situations you might not be able to dispense with but which you can modify a little. Although there might not be as much time as you would wish to spend on yourself, there could be an interesting encounter later in the day.

12 THURSDAY ☿   *Moon Age Day 6   Moon Sign Leo*

Planetary trends now favour a complete change in routine and, if possible, a change in location too. Those amongst you who have arranged to do something completely different today are the luckiest of all. What you need most of all is to stimulate your intellect, as well as that burning curiosity.

13 FRIDAY ☿ *Moon Age Day 7   Moon Sign Leo*

This ought to be a good day on the business front. Any new plan or scheme that is in your mind can be played out fairly successfully at the moment and especially so if you enlist the support of others. The only problems that could occur around this time do so if you try to go it alone too much.

14 SATURDAY ☿ *Moon Age Day 8   Moon Sign Leo*

Look out for interesting social possibilities and take some time out from the ordinary. It's absolutely essential for Sagittarians to get variety into their lives and to try new or alternative ways of doing things. Today you should be enjoying the company of people you find to be stimulating and intelligent.

15 SUNDAY ☿ *Moon Age Day 9   Moon Sign Virgo*

This is likely to be a day during which someone is responding positively to your romantic overtures. With everything to play for in a personal sense you show just how fascinating and intriguing you can be. There is a possibility that you will get somewhat quieter as the day advances.

16 MONDAY ☿ *Moon Age Day 10   Moon Sign Virgo*

It isn't likely to be everyday life that most appeals to you at the start of this working week but rather the odd or the unusual. Your curiosity is raised and the Archer definitely becomes a detective. It is the minutiae of life that appeals the most, together with working out exactly what makes others tick.

17 TUESDAY ☿ *Moon Age Day 11   Moon Sign Libra*

Beware of disagreements today and especially ones that are little more than a waste of time. It would be better to avoid getting on the wrong side of anyone if you can and you may need to be quite giving in order to accommodate the needs of family members. Friends should be easier to deal with.

18 WEDNESDAY ☿ *Moon Age Day 12   Moon Sign Libra*

You now have what it takes to push ahead on most fronts and although your powers of concentration are not all they might be, you can be sure of a good reception under most circumstances. Plan now for things you want to do later and make sure that most of these are going to be for pleasure.

19 THURSDAY ☿ *Moon Age Day 13 Moon Sign Libra*

The Archer seems to be quite restless right now and that is why it would be best to do something interesting rather than necessary today. You might get a lot from a shopping spree or a visit to somewhere that interests you intellectually. The deeper, more thoughtful, side of your mind demands your attention.

20 FRIDAY ☿ *Moon Age Day 14 Moon Sign Scorpio*

Look out for interesting social encounters and do what you can to mix business with pleasure. You won't take kindly to the need to devote every moment to practical matters and work best when you can show the humorous side of your Sagittarian nature. Your clowning gets you noticed.

21 SATURDAY ☿ *Moon Age Day 15 Moon Sign Scorpio*

The ability to assess how others are likely to behave under any given circumstance is a major skill for anyone, and trends suggest that you may have this today. You can make gains through your instinctive understanding of the way others are going to turn. Look towards the needs of your partner this weekend and show how much you care.

22 SUNDAY ☿ *Moon Age Day 16 Moon Sign Sagittarius*

This is a day during which you should take all your talents and put them to good use. Not only will you be very practical in your approach to life but you have everything you need to make gains that would have seemed unlikely only a few days ago. Get into gear as early as you can on this early summer Sunday.

23 MONDAY *Moon Age Day 17 Moon Sign Sagittarius*

Keep up the pressure and avoid getting involved with negative or awkward sorts of people. The path ahead seems to be strewn with blessings and you should be at your optimistic best. With general good luck on your side, this is the time of the month during which you can afford to take the odd chance.

24 TUESDAY *Moon Age Day 18 Moon Sign Sagittarius*

With everything to play for today you have what it takes to turn heads. This is Sagittarius at its social best and there are potential gains cropping up all the time as a result. Avoid unnecessary tasks and stick to what you know. This is the best way to further your ambitions, especially in a financial sense.

25 WEDNESDAY
Moon Age Day 19   Moon Sign Capricorn

You show an increased desire for travel and for broadening your horizons generally around this time. Active and enterprising, you are approaching new situations with a great sense of optimism and hope. When it comes to mixing with the world at large you show the very best qualities that the cheerful Archer has to offer.

26 THURSDAY
Moon Age Day 20   Moon Sign Capricorn

You feel the need to get along with everyone and although you will do your best to make sure this is the case, not everyone may be equally helpful. You might have to bend over backwards in order to accommodate awkward types but this is likely to do little to change your basically cheerful frame of mind.

27 FRIDAY
Moon Age Day 21   Moon Sign Aquarius

As the end of the working week approaches you may need to put something into action that will further your intentions next week. In some ways you are now slightly quieter and more contemplative and it is possible that someone you mix with most of the time might think you are down in the dumps.

28 SATURDAY
Moon Age Day 22   Moon Sign Aquarius

The outcome of a major decision made a few weeks ago now proves to be very rewarding. Keep a sense of proportion if you are at work and do what you can to lift the spirits of people who seem a bit down in the dumps. Routines can be quite comfortable and help you to live a more ordered sort of day.

29 SUNDAY
Moon Age Day 23   Moon Sign Pisces

You remain basically filled with enthusiasm and excitement for projects that capture your imagination. It seems as though you are on the edge of something important but it might be difficult working out exactly what that might be. Friends are good to have around and prove to be extremely entertaining.

30 MONDAY
Moon Age Day 24   Moon Sign Pisces

Do your best to explore the world this week and don't get so bogged down with everyday routines that you fail to notice what is happening around you. Conforming to expectations at work may not be easy, but this doesn't matter because it is your spontaneity that appeals to others.

31 TUESDAY
Moon Age Day 25   Moon Sign Pisces

Social trends still look good and you get a great deal of joy from all manner of encounters. This is especially true when you are dealing with people who have recently come into your life. Communications of all kinds prove to be vitally important today, even if they don't seem to be so at first.

June

2016

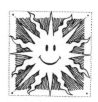

Your Month at a Glance

(+) = Opportunities are around   ⊖ = Be on the defensive   = Life is pretty ordinary

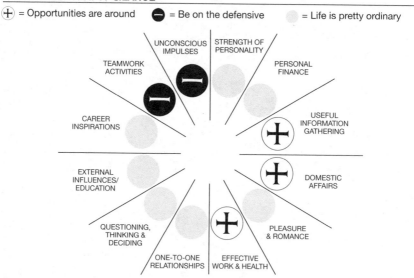

June Highs and Lows

Here I show you how the rhythms of the Moon will affect you this month. Like the tide, your energies and abilities will rise and fall with its pattern. When it is above the centre line, go for it, when it is below, you should be resting.

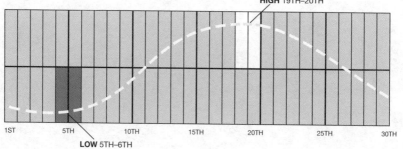

HIGH 19TH–20TH

LOW 5TH–6TH

I WEDNESDAY
Moon Age Day 26   Moon Sign Aries

It looks as though you will be very persuasive at the moment so if there is anything you really want, now is the time to ask for it. At the same time you should find your friends to be very supportive and willing to go that extra mile on your behalf. Popularity counts and you have plenty.

2 THURSDAY
Moon Age Day 27   Moon Sign Aries

The more you are out there amongst groups of people the better life is likely to work out for you. The Archer is nearly always gregarious and doesn't function for long on its own. You feel more comfortable as part of a team and it's especially good at the moment to bounce your ideas off others.

3 FRIDAY
Moon Age Day 28   Moon Sign Taurus

Decisions have to be made, even though life can sometimes be rather confusing. If you are not sure how to proceed, especially at work, this might be the time to listen to someone you respect. You can't know everything but there is a wealth of help out there if you are willing to admit that you need it.

4 SATURDAY
Moon Age Day 0   Moon Sign Taurus

The weekend has arrived and you might be very pleased to see it. You have had a busy week and now you need some time to do whatever takes your fancy. Perhaps you will opt for a shopping spree or a meeting of some sort with friends who are important to you? Whatever you decide, leave work alone for a while.

5 SUNDAY
Moon Age Day I   Moon Sign Gemini

Don't be in the least surprised if you suddenly find that you are lacking in self-belief and general confidence. The lunar low is going to cause you to slow down and may even be responsible for a little depression. As long as you realise that these matters are purely temporary, you will deal with them well.

6 MONDAY
Moon Age Day 2   Moon Sign Gemini

Another less-than-wonderful day is on the cards but how it turns out really depends on how you deal with situations. Be willing to watch and wait, whilst at the same time turning your mind towards matters you find stimulating or enjoyable. Action will lead to exhaustion, so stick to planning instead, if you can.

7 TUESDAY
Moon Age Day 3   Moon Sign Cancer

Progress might still not be all you would wish but if you analyse the situation carefully you will see that you are making headway, albeit quite slowly. If you accept the fact that you need to think things through, all should be well. Anything particularly old or unusual is inclined to attract your attention now.

8 WEDNESDAY
Moon Age Day 4   Moon Sign Cancer

Although you shouldn't be afraid to take the initiative, it is possible that something that seemed extremely important a couple of days ago will now lose its appeal. This is because your mind has moved on, something that is common with Sagittarians. Your originality, however, is really on display around now.

9 THURSDAY
Moon Age Day 5   Moon Sign Leo

You should have plenty of chance to make significant headway now but you might still show a tendency to be too rash for your own good. Try ideas out in your mind and work them through carefully before committing yourself in the real world. A theoretical failure is very much better than a real and costly one.

10 FRIDAY
Moon Age Day 6   Moon Sign Leo

You might not be able to move mountains today but it will be fun to try. With a mixture of ingenuity and subtlety there is very little that lies beyond your powers. Make use of this short but potent period in order to further your interests in almost any way you choose. Sporting activities could appeal to you now.

11 SATURDAY
Moon Age Day 7   Moon Sign Virgo

Most of what you want can be yours with a little effort. All the same you may be feeling slightly restless and will want to do something to prove to yourself that you are really alive. Friends can be quite inspirational at this time and your partner is also likely to have some very good ideas for dispelling the blues.

12 SUNDAY
Moon Age Day 8   Moon Sign Virgo

You won't have trouble attracting others at present and it looks as though your general popularity is higher than it has been for some time. This should please you no end because – whether or not you choose to admit it – you love to be loved. In work-based situations it is important to double-check details.

13 MONDAY
Moon Age Day 9   Moon Sign Virgo

Finding time to pay enough attention to family members, and in particular to your partner, might not be very easy at the start of what could turn out to be a busy week. Nevertheless it is important to make time, and just a few minutes with your arm around someone who is important to you is all it probably takes.

14 TUESDAY
Moon Age Day 10   Moon Sign Libra

You may find that not everyone is equally approachable today and the attitude of one or two people could leave you guessing. All the same this should be a happy sort of interlude and one during which you do more thinking than acting. Some Sagittarian people will be feeling in need of a holiday around now.

15 WEDNESDAY
Moon Age Day 11   Moon Sign Libra

Keep your ears open during the middle of this week because even casual conversations can carry information that proves to be both illuminating and of practical use. With the ability to modify the ideas of those around you, it looks as though you are particularly inventive at this stage of the month. This is a trend you can exploit.

16 THURSDAY
Moon Age Day 12   Moon Sign Scorpio

Your personal objectives could be taking a back seat for today because you seem to be spending most of your time working for others. This is especially true in the case of colleagues, some of whom are a little out of their depth and need your special touch. Surprise your partner this evening with a gift.

17 FRIDAY
Moon Age Day 13   Moon Sign Scorpio

You like to be doing more than one thing at a time and it is the very essence of the Sagittarian nature to get variety into life. A slightly slower interlude is almost certain whilst the Moon passes through your solar twelfth house but this will not prevent you from showing a cheerful face to the world.

18 SATURDAY
Moon Age Day 14   Moon Sign Scorpio

The need to find a simpler way forward seems to be emphasised by present trends. It could be that certain matters have become far more complicated than they should be. Slacken the pace a little and take some time out to think things through. A refreshing change at home may come this evening or tomorrow.

19 SUNDAY
Moon Age Day 15   Moon Sign Sagittarius

Now is the time to take all your enthusiasm and self-belief and to make it work on your behalf. The lunar high offers new incentives and also brings a period during which things seem to work out pretty much of their own accord. Stand by for an active day – and another one tomorrow.

20 MONDAY
Moon Age Day 16   Moon Sign Sagittarius

Don't wait to be asked today. You have everything it takes to achieve some longed-for objectives and you feel the need to be at the front of anything you consider to be important. You will completely fail to notice if one or two people are not on your side and you have so much self-belief it doesn't really matter.

21 TUESDAY
Moon Age Day 17   Moon Sign Capricorn

Open up to loved ones and spill the beans regarding something that has bothered you for a while. You are now in a position to clear the air and to get on side with those who don't always understand what motivates you. A calmer and more rational period on the home front is indicated by prevailing trends.

22 WEDNESDAY
Moon Age Day 18   Moon Sign Capricorn

There are plenty of good contacts around at the moment, and these are likely to have far more to do with the professional sphere of your life than the personal. Some frustrations will potentially crop up, mainly in the area of love. Avoid doing anything that provokes jealousy in others, particularly your partner.

23 THURSDAY
Moon Age Day 19   Moon Sign Aquarius

Your desire to help others is extremely well-marked right now and you have what it takes to get to the heart of a very difficult situation. You should discover your voice again, after a few days during which you might have been slightly quiet. When you do speak out, it is likely to be on behalf of the downtrodden.

24 FRIDAY
Moon Age Day 20   Moon Sign Aquarius

Keep your ears open today because there is some good advice about. The only difficulty here is that to accept what is being suggested you will need to make a change of direction. This in itself is not too much of a problem; the issue at stake is whether you are willing to eat a little humble pie.

25 SATURDAY
Moon Age Day 21   Moon Sign Aquarius

You have faith in your own abilities but might doubt that others have what it takes to keep up. There is a slightly ruthless streak around at the moment and though this isn't entirely unusual for Sagittarius, you do need to exercise a little caution. Major decisions really ought to wait for a day or two.

26 SUNDAY
Moon Age Day 22   Moon Sign Pisces

At the back of your mind there is a little place where excitement is mounting. It may be that you have a plan to do something rather unusual, or the germ of an idea that you just know is going to work out well. Spend some time getting to grips with family members who seem to be going slightly off the rails.

27 MONDAY
Moon Age Day 23   Moon Sign Pisces

Look out for a more important social dimension entering your life this week. There are some interesting possibilities likely as a result and the Archer should be right on the ball when it comes to seeing ahead and making the right moves. This is also likely to be a week during which romance figures heavily.

28 TUESDAY
Moon Age Day 24   Moon Sign Aries

It looks as though you will be more sensitive than usual to the casual remarks that are being made around you. Before you fly off the handle just make sure that these comments are definitely aimed in your direction. The Archer is just a little cranky at the moment and apt to be slightly irrational.

29 WEDNESDAY
Moon Age Day 25   Moon Sign Aries

It is towards the practical aspects of life that your mind is apt to turn at the moment and you could find that you are busy around the homestead, getting things sorted out to your satisfaction. You might have to make a few new starts but the achievements that come along as a result make the effort worthwhile.

30 THURSDAY
Moon Age Day 26   Moon Sign Taurus

You get on especially well today in situations that demand your full attention and your excellent ability to get a message across. In work situations you definitely lead from the front and will not expect anyone to do anything you are not willing to do yourself. Rules are important today, but not if they restrict you.

2016

YOUR MONTH AT A GLANCE

(+) = Opportunities are around ⬤ = Be on the defensive ⬤ = Life is pretty ordinary

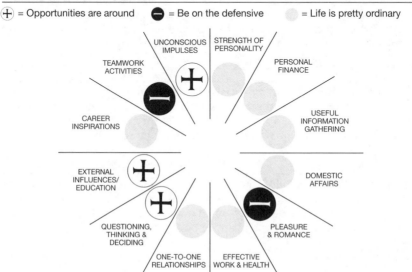

JULY HIGHS AND LOWS

Here I show you how the rhythms of the Moon will affect you this month. Like the tide, your energies and abilities will rise and fall with its pattern. When it is above the centre line, go for it, when it is below, you should be resting.

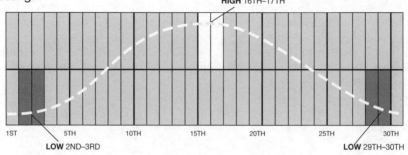

1 FRIDAY
Moon Age Day 27   Moon Sign Taurus

Although you may be quite busy with practical matters today it would be sensible to take time out to think about your love life. If things have not been going entirely according to plan in this area of life, now you have what it takes to do something about it. Comfort and security really seem to matter under present trends.

2 SATURDAY
Moon Age Day 28   Moon Sign Gemini

The lunar low might take the wind out of your sails a little but there are some very supportive planetary influences about and it's possible that these will totally overcome the adverse position of the Moon. This would not be a good day to become involved in arguments you can't hope to win.

3 SUNDAY
Moon Age Day 29   Moon Sign Gemini

Although things are likely to be going your way in a general sense you won't get everything your heart desires today. Accept that there is no point in slogging away at something you know is lost and instead turn your sights in new directions. Try to get some variety into your life if possible.

4 MONDAY
Moon Age Day 0   Moon Sign Cancer

Logic has its place in your life but so does gut instinct. You will probably be more inclined to follow the latter for much of the time today and can make gains as a result. Your judgement generally seems to be sound, even if there are people around now who have severe doubts about the conclusions you reach.

5 TUESDAY
Moon Age Day 1   Moon Sign Cancer

You want to keep busy but at the same time there are all sorts of distracting diversions around. For today you go through life like someone in a curiosity shop and you just can't get enough of the fascinating goods on offer. This is the real magic of the Sagittarian mind and it's part of what feeds your popularity.

6 WEDNESDAY
Moon Age Day 2   Moon Sign Leo

Domestic and family matters should prove to be essentially rewarding under present planetary trends and you probably won't be quite so committed to out-of-house jobs as would normally be the case. This would be an excellent time for Sagittarians to start planning a magical holiday.

7 THURSDAY
Moon Age Day 3   Moon Sign Leo

The Archer is never lacking in charm at any time, but under present planetary trends this quality seems to be stronger than ever. This is one of the best periods during July to get what you want – most of the time simply by asking. This should also be a rewarding phase for your personal finances.

8 FRIDAY
Moon Age Day 4   Moon Sign Virgo

If today feels as if the weekend should have arrived already, this is a signal that you may have been pushing yourself too hard in the recent past. Take some time out and, if possible, get right away from everyday routines. If this isn't possible, try to find ways in which you can share responsibilities more than you usually do.

9 SATURDAY
Moon Age Day 5   Moon Sign Virgo

Present astrological trends incline your mind to drift towards the past, and you may find yourself trying to put right something from long ago that you are not proud of. Although it's good that you care, you are likely to discover that the only sort of commitment that pays dividends is that to the present and future.

10 SUNDAY
Moon Age Day 6   Moon Sign Virgo

You need to work your way through what could seem like a mountain of red tape if you want to get ahead at the moment. The secret is to deal with one task at a time, rather than trying to do everything simultaneously; that way you manage to achieve what others are presently finding impossible.

11 MONDAY
Moon Age Day 7   Moon Sign Libra

Keep in touch with those you know have your best interests at heart, whilst at the same time spending at least some time with your partner. With popularity working for you, there isn't much that is beyond your abilities when it comes to social situations and you really shine in any intellectual or dramatic pursuit.

12 TUESDAY
Moon Age Day 8   Moon Sign Libra

Trends suggest that you will be in good spirits today. There is nobody better than the Archer when it comes to cheering up a gloomy soul and you have it within your power today to lift the mood of practically everyone you meet. This attitude alone can turn failure into glorious success.

13 WEDNESDAY
Moon Age Day 9   Moon Sign Scorpio

It is the broader aspects of life that you need to be looking at today. Don't concentrate your efforts in just one direction and also don't allow yourself to be tied down by mundane jobs. A light and bright approach works best and you should be quite captivated by the sort of attention you are getting from particular people.

14 THURSDAY
Moon Age Day 10   Moon Sign Scorpio

Your confidence is now on the rise and you display a very original and forward-looking attitude. Romantic matters are working well under present trends, and Sagittarians who are between relationships at this time should concentrate all their efforts in a single direction. Avoid being too touchy with friends.

15 FRIDAY
Moon Age Day 11   Moon Sign Scorpio

It is your originality that shines out at the moment along with that special inspirational quality that often sets the Archer apart. Your present efficiency should enable you to get to grips with a task that you haven't been looking forward to and get it out of the way in a flash. After that, simply enjoy the time of year.

16 SATURDAY
Moon Age Day 12   Moon Sign Sagittarius

It's time to follow up on any lead that looks promising and to put all your effort into getting ahead personally. The lunar high offers new incentives and enlivens your life no end. Confidence for some will be at an all-time high and you won't have to go far to uncover some real advantages.

17 SUNDAY
Moon Age Day 13   Moon Sign Sagittarius

The positive phase continues and if anything the pace increases. Whilst some people would be giddy with the possibilities that the present trends offer, the Archer is right in the groove and more than able to cope. Others find you attractive and are quite naturally willing to follow your lead.

18 MONDAY
Moon Age Day 14   Moon Sign Capricorn

Not everything that happens at the start of this week is likely to be working to your advantage, though you need to be careful because you can get the wrong impression. Even when others seem to be working against your best interests it is possible that they genuinely do know better than you do.

19 TUESDAY
Moon Age Day 15   Moon Sign Capricorn

New opportunities for employment seem to be on the horizon. Some Archers will be thinking in terms of an entirely new start, while some will be happy with an alteration to their present responsibilities. With friends you are warm and understanding and it is possible that a friendship could become much deeper for a few Sagittarians.

20 WEDNESDAY
Moon Age Day 16   Moon Sign Capricorn

You show considerable personal charm today when it matters the most and can get most of what you want simply by speaking the right words. Almost everyone is susceptible to this approach and will consequently go to great lengths to make you happy. Repaying this kindness is not at all difficult.

21 THURSDAY
Moon Age Day 17   Moon Sign Aquarius

It is towards the really original side of your nature that you turn today to discover the best way forward. Sagittarius is very creative at present and you may decide to embark upon specific changes at home that are going to make you feel more comfortable with your lot in life generally.

22 FRIDAY
Moon Age Day 18   Moon Sign Aquarius

At this time you work best when you are able to make your own decisions and you could feel just slightly restricted if messages from above restrict your actions in any way. With everything to play for in a romantic sense you should be able to pep up your love life no end, maybe by springing a surprise.

23 SATURDAY
Moon Age Day 19   Moon Sign Pisces

You might not be feeling exactly on top form and will be quite happy to potter along quietly and even to stay in the background more than would usually be the case. With a sense of impending mishaps, it is possible you will be taking actions that are really not necessary. You really should remain optimistic.

24 SUNDAY
Moon Age Day 20   Moon Sign Pisces

Once again you fail to be in the least captivated by the sort of things that Sunday has to offer. As a result you will almost certainly decide to turn your world upside down in some way. You need to enlist the support of family members who have a similar attitude because not everyone enjoys sudden breaks to their routines.

25 MONDAY
Moon Age Day 21   Moon Sign Aries

People who haven't figured in your life so far this year are likely to make a return visit. It may be that someone from far away is appearing or else you remember an individual who has been on the periphery of your life recently. Your attitude towards family matters might be seen as rather unusual now.

26 TUESDAY
Moon Age Day 22   Moon Sign Aries

This would be a good time to fix your attention on the medium and long-term and to think up new strategies that could see you better off than has been the case of late. Friends come good with their promises and are likely to offer timely assistance. Romance tends to be a more significant factor as the week advances.

27 WEDNESDAY
Moon Age Day 23   Moon Sign Taurus

Don't overlook those little details that can make all the difference to your ultimate success. This is especially true at work but the trend also spills over into your home life. It is the apparently inconsequential matters that need the most concentration and which assure you of getting on well for the next few days.

28 THURSDAY
Moon Age Day 24   Moon Sign Taurus

Stand by the decisions you have made but not to the point that it becomes necessary to fall out with anyone. If you need to make slight alterations in order to keep the peace, then that's the way it has to be. There might be some frustration caused by altered plans but at least you remain popular.

29 FRIDAY
Moon Age Day 25   Moon Sign Gemini

What goes on around you at home should be heart-warming and more than interesting. For this reason alone you could be abandoning any thought of real practical progress today and will be spending most of your time concerned with family matters. A shopping spree might also be good.

30 SATURDAY
Moon Age Day 26   Moon Sign Gemini

The Archer shows itself to be quite selfless today and much of what you do is for the direct benefit of others. Your social conscience is aroused, which could lead you to deal with issues in your local community or with local politics. You can be quite argumentative, in a constructive way, right now.

31 SUNDAY

Your sense of fair play is once again much emphasised and this could lead you to be very protective in the case of family members and friends. Sunday should be quite a happy day with plenty to keep you busy, and no matter what you are doing or who you do it with you should be left feeling happy.

2016

YOUR MONTH AT A GLANCE

⊕ = Opportunities are around ⬤ = Be on the defensive ⬤ = Life is pretty ordinary

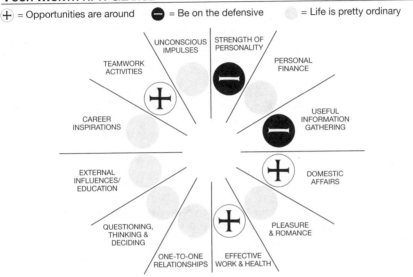

AUGUST HIGHS AND LOWS

Here I show you how the rhythms of the Moon will affect you this month. Like the tide, your energies and abilities will rise and fall with its pattern. When it is above the centre line, go for it, when it is below, you should be resting.

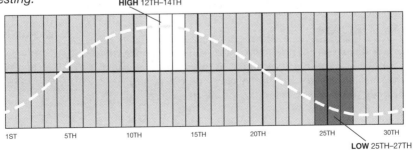

91

1 MONDAY
Moon Age Day 28   Moon Sign Cancer

With the prospect of a good day – and a week of possibilities – before you, today should start positively and you won't have any difficulty keeping busy. Don't get bogged down with issues that are of no real importance and, where possible, allow others to take some of the strain and to tackle the less interesting jobs.

2 TUESDAY
Moon Age Day 0   Moon Sign Cancer

There could be misunderstandings and disagreements to deal with, especially early in the day. Get through these as quickly as you can because the general trends are very good. Someone you know very well is in the market for some sound advice and you must take their problems seriously.

3 WEDNESDAY
Moon Age Day 1   Moon Sign Leo

You want to get as much done as you can at work and have what it takes to overturn difficulties from the past. Your mind is ingenious and although you are dealing with matters in a far from conventional way, you know how to succeed. A romantic encounter is not out of the question at this stage of the week.

4 THURSDAY
Moon Age Day 2   Moon Sign Leo

Although you could be in for one or two disappointments at the moment you should manage to cope with these very well. Present trends show the Archer maintaining a good sense of humour and that can help in every area of your life. Don't be too quick to judge the actions of someone you meet around now.

5 FRIDAY
Moon Age Day 3   Moon Sign Virgo

Stay as close to your friends as possible today. People at work who are also buddies have the recipe you need to push ahead and the more you talk to them, the more you become aware of this fact. The odd family problem can be resolved by talking things through in a rational manner.

6 SATURDAY
Moon Age Day 4   Moon Sign Virgo

You should avoid a tendency towards self-indulgence this weekend. Austerity is not necessary but you often try to experience too much and all at the same time. Simple is best for the Archer right now and you will actively enjoy dumping a few of the trappings of life that often only get in the way.

7 SUNDAY
Moon Age Day 5   Moon Sign Libra

Sunday could bring you closer to your heart's desire in some way and you need to be as active as possible if you are going to get the very best from what is on offer. You might be better off thinking in terms of enjoyment rather than advancement and you exhibit an especially attentive response to family members and friends.

8 MONDAY
Moon Age Day 6   Moon Sign Libra

Although you can't expect everything to go your way right now, when it matters most you come up with the goods. Life is not good for you simply because of any sort of luck. Most of the opportunities that come your way at the moment are as a direct result of the way you interact with situations.

9 TUESDAY
Moon Age Day 7   Moon Sign Libra

Slow down the action just a little today – not because you find it hard to cope but simply for the reason that you need to concentrate if you really want to forge ahead. Although it is the Sagittarian way to mix business with pleasure it would be best under prevailing trends to keep the two essentially separate.

10 WEDNESDAY
Moon Age Day 8   Moon Sign Scorpio

Today brings a new chance to make a favourable impression on someone you see as being quite significant. Don't be too quick to take offence at a remark that isn't intended to upset you and shrug off any small criticisms that come from others. Keep your mind on the matters you know to be most important.

11 THURSDAY
Moon Age Day 9   Moon Sign Scorpio

Use care and good judgement today and don't try to push ahead too much. By tomorrow the lunar high comes along, which will bring a much more positive phase but for the moment you will have to be patient. Opt for quiet pursuits and spend some time planning for events that lie ahead of you.

12 FRIDAY
Moon Age Day 10   Moon Sign Sagittarius

A much better day lies in store for you and the lunar high brings greater enthusiasm into your life generally. You know instinctively what you want and how to get it and there should be some significant good luck about now. With a great sense of confidence and purpose, you will enjoy great popularity.

13 SATURDAY
Moon Age Day 11   Moon Sign Sagittarius

With determination to stride ahead and a feeling that things are generally going your way, this is the time of the month to make progress. At work you should enjoy significant achievements whilst at the same time you may find that others are falling over themselves to follow your lead.

14 SUNDAY
Moon Age Day 12   Moon Sign Sagittarius

The light-hearted phase continues and the best qualities of the Archer are quite clearly on display. You probably won't take anything very seriously and find yourself almost catapulted into exciting situations. What you make of them is entirely up to you but there isn't any doubt about your enthusiasm.

15 MONDAY
Moon Age Day 13   Moon Sign Capricorn

Things generally seem to have reached an important phase and this is likely to be particularly true at work, or in any matter to do with education. Stick to the point when you have to sort out details and don't be diverted by the opinions of people you don't trust or who have proved to be unreliable in the past.

16 TUESDAY
Moon Age Day 14   Moon Sign Capricorn

Is Sagittarius really being socially reticent today? The fact is that you are not as friendly as would normally be the case and the stupidity of certain other people is really getting on your nerves. You won't want to show this to others, though, so there are times today when it would be best to stop and count to ten.

17 WEDNESDAY
Moon Age Day 15   Moon Sign Aquarius

Stand by for a fairly smooth-running sort of day, although not a period during which finances are likely to be especially strong. This won't matter too much because the sort of things that interest you at the moment are unlikely to cost you very much. Keep a sense of proportion regarding minor spats in the family.

18 THURSDAY
Moon Age Day 16   Moon Sign Aquarius

You may well be turning towards pet projects today and will be quite happy to potter along steadily. There could be sight complications in family matters or in discussions with colleagues. Gains can be made by remaining steadfast but not to the point that you become too fixed in your attitude.

19 FRIDAY
Moon Age Day 17   Moon Sign Pisces

Communication matters are positively highlighted at this time and you can get more or less anything you want by simply asking in the right way. At the same time you should find that romance is blossoming nicely, especially so in the case of Archers who have recently found a new love.

20 SATURDAY
Moon Age Day 18   Moon Sign Pisces

Energy should be used sparingly today, not because there is any lack of it but on account of the fact that concentration brings its own rewards. You seem to instinctively understand the thoughts and motivations of others and will be very pleased to offer timely assistance to family members and friends.

21 SUNDAY
Moon Age Day 19   Moon Sign Aries

There ought to be a great sense of personal rejuvenation around now and you will be quite willing to turn your world upside down if that is what it takes to get your way. The same probably cannot be said for those with whom you live and just a little understanding of their situation on your part would be welcome.

22 MONDAY
Moon Age Day 20   Moon Sign Aries

Material concerns will most likely be on your mind at the beginning of this week and it is clear that you want to get things done, even if others prove a little tardy in keeping up. Later in the day you may run out of steam but this is only because you are probably trying to achieve too much.

23 TUESDAY
Moon Age Day 21   Moon Sign Taurus

Some care will be necessary with regard to specific decisions and especially ones that have a personal or a romantic dimension. Spend the day with loved ones if you can and allow the traces of responsibility to fall for just a few hours. Your demonstrations of affection will be most welcome.

24 WEDNESDAY
Moon Age Day 22   Moon Sign Taurus

You might be slightly preoccupied with the past for a day or two, which is fairly unusual for your zodiac sign. There's nothing wrong with this, except the realisation on your part that what really matters is the present and the future. Some small frustrations could crop up later in the day.

25 THURSDAY
Moon Age Day 23   Moon Sign Gemini

You have to deal with the lunar low today and tomorrow so it would be best if you were to avoid too much in the way of pointless or fruitless activity. Simply concentrate on what matters the most to you and allow others to sort out their own messes for once. The chances are that you will remain generally cheerful.

26 FRIDAY
Moon Age Day 24   Moon Sign Gemini

An enforced lay-off doesn't suit you at all but that's what you will probably have to deal with today. Do what is necessary but apart from that it would be best to spend some time doing things that please you. Despite the position of the Moon you remain chatty, generally committed and you are well able to plan ahead.

27 SATURDAY
Moon Age Day 25   Moon Sign Gemini

You probably won't be expressing yourself quite as clearly as you would wish, though this may have little to do with your personality and is more a reflection of the fact that some people simply are not listening. If you have to repeat yourself too many times you could easily get cranky.

28 SUNDAY
Moon Age Day 26   Moon Sign Cancer

Life needs to be an open book for you right now. Leave aside all complications and keep things just as simple as you can. In your approach to others you need to be honest. If you are, they will understand you instantly and misunderstandings will not take place. This is a good day for making major purchases.

29 MONDAY
Moon Age Day 27   Moon Sign Cancer

New ideas and fresh starts seem to be the order of the day. Avoid pointless routines and concentrate on matters that please you personally. Also avoid acting too much on impulse, even though this is a tall order for the Archer. The more organised you are now, the better you play into the hands of present astrological trends.

30 TUESDAY
Moon Age Day 28   Moon Sign Leo

There are trends around today that favour financial prosperity and which see you slightly better off than you may have expected at this time of the month. It could be that you are simply proving to be luckier than usual but it is also possible that something you did in the past now begins to pay dividends.

31 WEDNESDAY ☿   *Moon Age Day 29   Moon Sign Leo*

There are many challenges around today but that is a very positive thing as far as you are concerned and simply brings new incentives when they prove to be most welcome. Don't get too obsessed with details, especially at work because it is the overview of life that matters the most at the moment.

September 2016

Your Month at a Glance

(+) = Opportunities are around   ● = Be on the defensive   ○ = Life is pretty ordinary

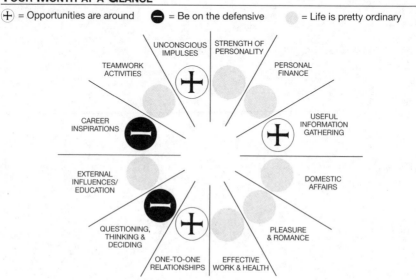

UNCONSCIOUS IMPULSES

STRENGTH OF PERSONALITY

TEAMWORK ACTIVITIES

PERSONAL FINANCE

CAREER INSPIRATIONS

USEFUL INFORMATION GATHERING

EXTERNAL INFLUENCES/ EDUCATION

DOMESTIC AFFAIRS

QUESTIONING, THINKING & DECIDING

PLEASURE & ROMANCE

ONE-TO-ONE RELATIONSHIPS

EFFECTIVE WORK & HEALTH

September Highs and Lows

Here I show you how the rhythms of the Moon will affect you this month. Like the tide, your energies and abilities will rise and fall with its pattern. When it is above the centre line, go for it, when it is below, you should be resting.

HIGH 9TH–10TH

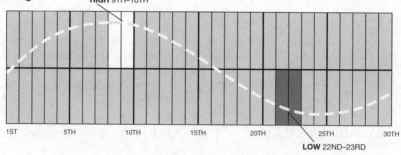

1ST   5TH   10TH   15TH   20TH   25TH   30TH

LOW 22ND–23RD

98

1 THURSDAY   ☿   *Moon Age Day 0   Moon Sign Virgo*

You seem to be right on the ball now when it comes to communicating, though of course there's nothing very strange about that as far as the Archer is concerned. Your interests appear to be topical and if you are an older Sagittarian you may feel that without any effort on your part you are coming back into fashion again.

2 FRIDAY   ☿   *Moon Age Day 1   Moon Sign Virgo*

Get on side with people you know have some good ideas. Teamwork is especially well highlighted under present trends and you won't have to look far to find something extremely interesting to do. It could be that the Archer is really feeling the need for some fresh air around this time.

3 SATURDAY   ☿   *Moon Age Day 2   Moon Sign Virgo*

It's rarely difficult for you to see the point of view of someone else but you could be very stretched to do so today. Most likely it won't be your fault and you can't be expected to follow the twists and turns of every single individual. As long as you stay patient and keep your sense of humour all should be well.

4 SUNDAY   ☿   *Moon Age Day 3   Moon Sign Libra*

What makes today a little strange is just how many people are turning to you for help and advice. In at least one situation you might be inclined to be a little sceptical and even suspicious. It's good to be on your guard but you are most likely seeing potential problems that don't really exist at all.

5 MONDAY   ☿   *Moon Age Day 4   Moon Sign Libra*

It can't be denied that there are likely to be a few issues to be resolved today. The best way forward is to talk things through with the people concerned as you won't get anywhere by hiding things. Absolute truthfulness is imperative – unless of course you sense instinctively that it would be best to sugar the pill.

6 TUESDAY   ☿   *Moon Age Day 5   Moon Sign Scorpio*

It may well occur to you at the moment that things are only inclined to go wrong when you rush at them. It is usually something of a waste of time to tell Sagittarian people to slow down and to take matters one step at a time but this would be timely advice under present astrological trends.

7 WEDNESDAY ☿ *Moon Age Day 6 Moon Sign Scorpio*

If you are in charge of anything, today requires you to prove yourself in no uncertain terms. This may mean having to be rather more stern and commanding than would normally be the case, but if so you can blame the attitude of others. Even the Archer needs to lay down the law now and again.

8 THURSDAY ☿ *Moon Age Day 7 Moon Sign Scorpio*

Today is all about balance, which becomes necessary in a number of different ways. For example, there is the balance between commitment to friends and social situations and commitment to your partner and family members. Avoid any sort of extremes and today should go swimmingly.

9 FRIDAY ☿ *Moon Age Day 8 Moon Sign Sagittarius*

After what might seem like a slow start, today is likely to go off like a veritable rocket. The lunar high shows your winning ways amplified and you have exactly what it takes to get others to do your bidding. Not only can you feather your own nest today but you are also working hard for others.

10 SATURDAY ☿ *Moon Age Day 9 Moon Sign Sagittarius*

The positive trends continue and you will be able to stretch your mind in all sorts of new directions at the moment. It appears that your capacity for hard work is noteworthy but you rarely notice the effort. Social trends are also beneficial and you will be especially exciting when out and about with friends.

11 SUNDAY ☿ *Moon Age Day 10 Moon Sign Capricorn*

The major emphasis for this Sunday is on having fun. You can enlist the support of relatives or friends and might decide that your partner needs cheering up or spoiling in some way. Whatever you decide to do, it's an odds-on certainty that you will undertake it with every fibre of your being.

12 MONDAY ☿ *Moon Age Day 11 Moon Sign Capricorn*

Your desire to get ahead is likely to receive its own rewards today, even if life is somewhat frantic. There are certain situations in which you feel as though you are holding on by your fingertips but you need to keep faith with yourself and others. Stand by for the highly social period that is now in the offing.

13 TUESDAY ☿
Moon Age Day 12   Moon Sign Aquarius

Keep up the pressure but understand that your way forward isn't the same as that of everyone else. There are gains to be made in friendships and as a result of closer attachments. It is possible that you will be receiving some sort of attention that you could find to be just a little embarrassing.

14 WEDNESDAY ☿
Moon Age Day 13   Moon Sign Aquarius

Avoid confrontations of any sort. These are not necessary and will only cause confusion. For once it would be better to give in than to push issues so far they become ridiculous. Money matters should ease and you could even discover you are rather better off than you suspected.

15 THURSDAY ☿
Moon Age Day 14   Moon Sign Aquarius

There are financial gains to be made today and some of these could come like a bolt from the blue. Don't be too quick to jump to conclusions in matters of love or you could find yourself in a slightly embarrassing position. Sometimes the things that are never said turn out to be the most significant.

16 FRIDAY ☿
Moon Age Day 15   Moon Sign Pisces

You may have a few doubts about people who appear to know everything about a particular subject and will want to do some investigating for yourself. Friends are likely to be warm and will offer the greatest solace when the cares of the day are out of the way. Spend some time with a really good pal.

17 SATURDAY ☿
Moon Age Day 16   Moon Sign Pisces

There are signs that you may be coming to the end of a particular phase of your life and the time is right to look ahead for something new. This is unlikely to have a bearing on relationships and seems to be an entirely practical matter. Sort out your finances and get all those bits of paper into some sort of order.

18 SUNDAY ☿
Moon Age Day 17   Moon Sign Aries

You don't have your usual ability to deal with practical matters in an efficient way, which is why you might have to call on the good offices of someone in the know. This is not necessarily a bad thing because you can go up in the estimation of a superior especially if you show that you are willing to learn.

19 MONDAY ☿ *Moon Age Day 18   Moon Sign Aries*

What you show more than anything today is a tendency to be resourceful. You know what you want from life and have some very good ideas about how approach the world. Don't be too quick to tell someone else they are wrong. A little diplomacy works best, no matter how sure you are of yourself.

20 TUESDAY ☿ *Moon Age Day 19   Moon Sign Taurus*

Just being what you naturally are is enough to get you noticed right now. There may be some slight difficulties during today but these are likely to be caused by the insensitivity of others, mainly family members. You may be called upon to sort out a dispute that you see as being entirely stupid.

21 WEDNESDAY ☿ *Moon Age Day 20   Moon Sign Taurus*

There are influences around now that definitely quicken your mind and which find you well able to address issues that could have confused you in the past. Energy levels are increasing and you won't have much difficulty dealing with a person who has given you problems in the past.

22 THURSDAY *Moon Age Day 21   Moon Sign Gemini*

Instead of trying to force issues today you need to simply leave some matters alone. Don't worry, the saucepan of life is still simmering, even if you find this difficult to believe for the moment. The Archer needs to remain cheerful and optimistic, while realising that the present trends are nothing more than a temporary hiccup.

23 FRIDAY *Moon Age Day 22   Moon Sign Gemini*

Try to avoid being stubborn and take on board the ideas and incentives put forward by people you trust. Not everyone is on your side right now but things might look slightly darker than they really are because the present position of the Moon is making you far more pessimistic than would normally be the case.

24 SATURDAY *Moon Age Day 23   Moon Sign Cancer*

Not everyone can keep up with your thought processes at the moment and you may have to keep slowing down in order to accommodate colleagues. You would be in a good position to impress a boss but you should avoid giving the impression that you know everything – even when you are sure you do.

25 SUNDAY
Moon Age Day 24   Moon Sign Cancer

All types of travel, together with cultural diversions, promise to lift the quality of your Sunday. Things can happen very quickly at the moment but thinking on your feet is second nature and doesn't give you any real problem. There could be slight financial gains in the offing, maybe as a result of simple good luck.

26 MONDAY
Moon Age Day 25   Moon Sign Leo

There is a strong emphasis on financial security and a need for you to count the pennies today, even though it is not necessary to do so. There is a positive side to this because you can get some real bargains while you are willing to look around and to barter. People generally approach you in a fair way.

27 TUESDAY
Moon Age Day 26   Moon Sign Leo

Everyday affairs should be looking generally settled but if there is nothing especially exciting going on you will have to do something about this yourself. It may seem that one particular task is taking forever but you could get it out of the way quicker if you were willing to enlist some help.

28 WEDNESDAY
Moon Age Day 27   Moon Sign Virgo

It looks as though you will be making a push for even greater freedom today and you could get on the wrong side of others as a result. The way forward is to show a greater understanding of those around you and not to cross them simply for the sake of it. The Archer can sometimes be an unintentional bully.

29 THURSDAY
Moon Age Day 28   Moon Sign Virgo

The present planetary picture offers every opportunity for personal rewards, which is why you will be chancing your arm more than usual. Don't get tied up in red tape regarding any family decision that has to be made and if you don't understand what the small print says, avoid signing any document.

30 FRIDAY
Moon Age Day 0   Moon Sign Virgo

Your willpower is legendary and there are few people around at the moment who can match you in anything, at least not once you have really set your mind to something. Don't be too quick to criticise people in the family or good friends. Someone else may leap to their defence and cause you real problems.

October
2016

Your Month at a Glance

$\oplus$ = Opportunities are around　　$\ominus$ = Be on the defensive　　⬤ = Life is pretty ordinary

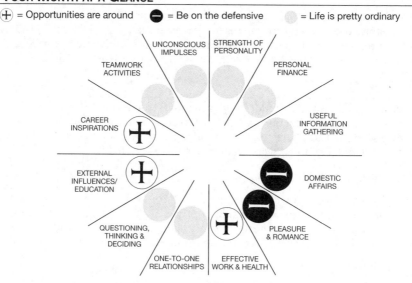

UNCONSCIOUS IMPULSES

STRENGTH OF PERSONALITY

TEAMWORK ACTIVITIES

PERSONAL FINANCE

CAREER INSPIRATIONS

USEFUL INFORMATION GATHERING

EXTERNAL INFLUENCES/ EDUCATION

DOMESTIC AFFAIRS

QUESTIONING, THINKING & DECIDING

PLEASURE & ROMANCE

ONE-TO-ONE RELATIONSHIPS

EFFECTIVE WORK & HEALTH

October Highs and Lows

Here I show you how the rhythms of the Moon will affect you this month. Like the tide, your energies and abilities will rise and fall with its pattern. When it is above the centre line, go for it, when it is below, you should be resting.

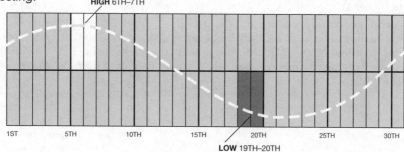

HIGH 6TH–7TH

1ST　　5TH　　10TH　　15TH　　20TH　　25TH　　30TH

LOW 19TH–20TH

104

1 SATURDAY
Moon Age Day 1   Moon Sign Libra

What probably matters the most at present is your ability to explain things to others. This is a unique gift and comes about because you have a chameleon-like ability to adapt to circumstances. There might be several different Sagittarians on offer today and each of them is specifically geared towards a particular situation.

2 SUNDAY
Moon Age Day 2   Moon Sign Libra

Relationships should be especially rewarding around now as a quieter quality descends on your general mood. You can take most matters in your stride and may choose to handle Sunday quietly. With a very different and inspirational new week in view, a few hours to please yourself today won't go amiss.

3 MONDAY
Moon Age Day 3   Moon Sign Scorpio

With just a little luck and a good following wind you can achieve something now that has been on your mind for quite a while. Use your natural ingenuity and also enlist the support of a willing volunteer if necessary. It would be quite sensible to keep quiet about a secret that is doing the rounds at present.

4 TUESDAY
Moon Age Day 4   Moon Sign Scorpio

Routines can be very boring to the average Sagittarian and that's one reason why you will probably be avoiding them today. You want to do things your own way and that could mean overturning conventions. That's fine but you need to be careful not to tread on the toes of someone else whilst you are at it.

5 WEDNESDAY
Moon Age Day 5   Moon Sign Scorpio

You never know who or what is going to turn up and, to be quite honest, that's the way you prefer life to be. Active and enterprising, you throw yourself into a fairly hectic Wednesday but should find a great deal of support when it matters the most. Standard romantic responses might not be enough at present.

6 THURSDAY
Moon Age Day 6   Moon Sign Sagittarius

Keeping ahead of the game is always important to you but rarely more so than it is today. With a perfect combination of common sense and intuition, you won't have to work too hard to score some significant successes. The lunar high keeps you focused on the matter at hand.

7 FRIDAY

Moon Age Day 7   Moon Sign Sagittarius

Things are likely to be as good as they get at home and you might find yourself in a position to spend more time with those you care about the most. Despite this fact you remain essentially committed to new projects and will be quite certain of your opinions and actions whilst astrological trends remain the way they are now.

8 SATURDAY

Moon Age Day 8   Moon Sign Capricorn

You should not be too surprised to realise just how popular you are at the moment – after all you work hard at life and have naturally winning ways. Even the most casual remarks made by others can have deeper meanings than seems to be the case at first so it's worth keeping your ears open.

9 SUNDAY

Moon Age Day 9   Moon Sign Capricorn

With plenty to play for and one of the most potentially satisfying Sundays of the year at your command, this is a day to make the most of every possible opportunity. You tend to be calm and relaxed, even when life around you seems to be very hectic. The Archer is in a strange frame of mind but others may find it electrifying.

10 MONDAY

Moon Age Day 10   Moon Sign Capricorn

A natural restlessness keeps you on the go today. Your mind is ingenious, electric and different. These are qualities that get you noticed and which ensure your continued popularity with individuals and groups. Don't be afraid to say what you think today because people genuinely want to listen.

11 TUESDAY

Moon Age Day 11   Moon Sign Aquarius

It isn't towards today or tomorrow that your mind is turning now but rather to the longer-term future. This is fairly unusual for you because you are generally a child of the moment. However, there is no harm whatsoever in maintaining a longer and broader view and you should take advantage of this present state of mind.

12 WEDNESDAY

Moon Age Day 12   Moon Sign Aquarius

With the Archer now at its most inventive you find ways to bring situations round to your advantage. Pep up your romantic life by arranging something you know will please your partner or lover and also find the time to talk an important matter through with a family member.

13 THURSDAY
Moon Age Day 13   Moon Sign Pisces

Life can be fairly unpredictable right now but this puts you at a significant advantage. Nobody is better at thinking on their feet than you are and you can forge successes out of the most moderate possibilities. Relationships should be uppermost in your mind under present trends, especially those of a romantic nature.

14 FRIDAY
Moon Age Day 14   Moon Sign Pisces

Impulsive thinking on your part can lead to misunderstandings. So powerful is your desire for change and diversity that you may find it hard to explain yourself when it is most necessary. Taking just a few minutes to get your point of view across to others is definitely worthwhile and could avoid problems later.

15 SATURDAY
Moon Age Day 15   Moon Sign Aries

Although not everyone has your best interests at heart your intuition should be strong enough at the moment to let you know who is worthy of your trust. There is great warmth in personal attachments for this Saturday and maybe enough time to say those things that often get over-looked in a busy life.

16 SUNDAY
Moon Age Day 16   Moon Sign Aries

In a social sense you need change and even if it doesn't seem to come along of its own volition you can change things by your own actions. In some ways your mind is now committed to the past, which can bring warm memories but not much in the way of practical help. Keep your mind on the future when you can.

17 MONDAY
Moon Age Day 17   Moon Sign Taurus

You will probably be looking closely at family finances right now. It isn't very long until Christmas and if you do some judicious spending right now you could save some money in the longer-term. It is the essence of your nature at the moment to look well ahead and to be filled with exciting plans.

18 TUESDAY
Moon Age Day 18   Moon Sign Taurus

If at all possible you need to put a full stop to a particular issue that has been on your mind for a while now. The planets are in the right position for you to make new starts and to look at situations with a very new attitude. Spend some time with your partner and enjoy what romance has to offer at this fortunate time.

19 WEDNESDAY   *Moon Age Day 19   Moon Sign Gemini*

The middle of this working week won't be the best imaginable period, and with the lunar low hovering about you will need all your ingenuity to get things done. Because you are slightly lacking in energy you need to be careful about what you decide to take on and even then you could do with some timely assistance.

20 THURSDAY   *Moon Age Day 20   Moon Sign Gemini*

Another slightly lack-lustre day is possible but there are still gains around if you choose to look carefully for them. Ignore the difficulties caused by people who seem determined to be awkward, if only because you may be unintentionally contributing to the problems yourself. Take some rest.

21 FRIDAY   *Moon Age Day 21   Moon Sign Cancer*

You need to exercise a little sense where money is concerned and to avoid spending lavishly on things you don't really need at all. There are some gains around in terms of your romantic life but these tend to come despite you rather than because of you. Take benefits where they are offered and don't question them.

22 SATURDAY   *Moon Age Day 22   Moon Sign Cancer*

Your intuition is heightened around now and you should not turn away from those important little messages that crop up at the back of your mind. You should know instinctively who you can trust and who should be left alone. Following the advice of a friend could lead to a small financial gain.

23 SUNDAY   *Moon Age Day 23   Moon Sign Leo*

There are rewards coming along in the financial sphere and you have what you need to get ahead in terms of your work. If there is any fly in the ointment at the moment it might come from family members, some of whom seem to be less than happy with their lot and may be expressing this fact.

24 MONDAY   *Moon Age Day 24   Moon Sign Leo*

New opportunities look good but you may find you are inclined to be slightly lazier than usual. What will really appeal to you is luxury in one form or another and it is clear that under present trends you are happy to be pampered. In a social sense you look and feel right, which is why you are noticed.

25 TUESDAY
Moon Age Day 25   Moon Sign Leo

Thinking is much intensified today and you may spend more time mulling things over than you do applying yourself. This is not necessarily a bad thing because there are periods during which you need to batter your ideas into shape before you make a start in a practical sense. The action comes a little further down the road.

26 WEDNESDAY
Moon Age Day 26   Moon Sign Virgo

Even common-or-garden routines can seem more interesting under present trends and you undertake menial tasks with a greater willingness than usual. What seems to appeal to you most today is not so much what you do, but how you do it. Your general view is a longer-term one over the next few days.

27 THURSDAY
Moon Age Day 27   Moon Sign Virgo

You could have a significant difference of opinion with someone now, and you may have to agree to differ. This is certainly better than arguing. Under present trends little or nothing is gained by falling out with anyone and this is especially true at work. Spend some time in the evening doing just what takes your fancy.

28 FRIDAY
Moon Age Day 28   Moon Sign Libra

If you want to enjoy personal rewards today you will have to put in that extra bit of effort that can make all the difference. The fact is that you are right on the edge of something very important. All that is required now is the final push, plus a belief in your own ideas.

29 SATURDAY
Moon Age Day 29   Moon Sign Libra

Although you are now more than willing to make sacrifices for your friends, what is demanded of you could be just too great. Rather than doing too much for them, you should be willing to accept their offers of help. Don't get involved in financial deals at the moment, at least not unless you are absolutely sure of yourself.

30 SUNDAY
Moon Age Day 0   Moon Sign Libra

There's no doubt about it, Sagittarius is extremely curious right now. You want to know what makes everything tick and won't be happy to settle for compromises. In matters of love you are cheerful and co-operative, and may be undertaking little tasks that you know will please your partner.

31 MONDAY

Moon Age Day 1   Moon Sign Scorpio

Be ready to make allowances for others today because you can't really proceed without them. This could mean having to slow down in order to let colleagues catch up. At home you are less responsive to the general needs of loved ones, particularly so in the case of your partner.

November
2016

Your Month at a Glance

(+) = Opportunities are around   (–) = Be on the defensive   = Life is pretty ordinary

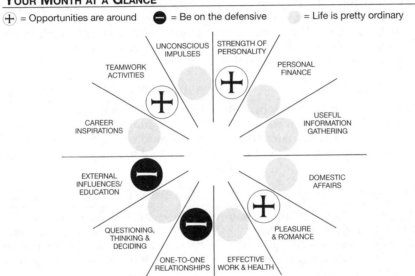

- UNCONSCIOUS IMPULSES
- STRENGTH OF PERSONALITY (+)
- TEAMWORK ACTIVITIES (+)
- PERSONAL FINANCE
- CAREER INSPIRATIONS
- USEFUL INFORMATION GATHERING
- EXTERNAL INFLUENCES/EDUCATION (–)
- DOMESTIC AFFAIRS
- QUESTIONING, THINKING & DECIDING (–)
- PLEASURE & ROMANCE (+)
- ONE-TO-ONE RELATIONSHIPS
- EFFECTIVE WORK & HEALTH

November Highs and Lows

Here I show you how the rhythms of the Moon will affect you this month. Like the tide, your energies and abilities will rise and fall with its pattern. When it is above the centre line, go for it, when it is below, you should be resting.

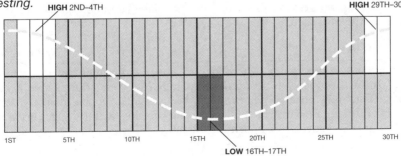

HIGH 2ND–4TH   HIGH 29TH–30TH

1ST   5TH   10TH   15TH   20TH   25TH   30TH

LOW 16TH–17TH

1 TUESDAY
Moon Age Day 2   Moon Sign Scorpio

Leave room for new plans and schemes because there is plenty happening at the moment and you need to be on the ball if you want to make the most of the opportunities that are presented. You might have to do something you hate and if so get it out of the way as early in the day as possible.

2 WEDNESDAY
Moon Age Day 3   Moon Sign Sagittarius

The lunar high should find you in a very positive frame of mind and willing to have a go at anything – even things you have turned your nose up at in the past. Who knows, you might enjoy yourself much more than you expected? Even if you don't, you get a certain satisfaction that comes from making other people happy.

3 THURSDAY
Moon Age Day 4   Moon Sign Sagittarius

Getting any form of rest is probably right out of the window today. This stage of the working week is apt to be demanding but very enjoyable. If you have any mountains to move, this would be the best time to get the shovel out. There could be some unexpected meetings at some stage later in the day.

4 FRIDAY
Moon Age Day 5   Moon Sign Sagittarius

This is not the best time of month to be gambling but if you really must take a chance it is important that your risks are calculated. Some limitations are placed upon you by life itself and you have to realise that it isn't always possible to have exactly what you want. Stay cool in tight situations.

5 SATURDAY
Moon Age Day 6   Moon Sign Capricorn

Though mentally alert and anxious to do whatever it takes to prove yourself, the best trends today are definitely personal ones. Attitude is very important when it comes to getting the best from romance and you should start with some overblown gesture, like a box of chocolates, a bunch of flowers or a ticket to the next match.

6 SUNDAY
Moon Age Day 7   Moon Sign Capricorn

A good lift comes along where one-to-one relationships are concerned and you will probably be concentrating much of your efforts in securing and maintaining positive relationships. You could do worse than to heap attention on your partner or the person you care for the most. This evening should prove particularly opportune for love.

7 MONDAY
Moon Age Day 8   Moon Sign Aquarius

If there are mysteries about at this time it's clear that you will want to solve them. Sagittarius the detective makes another appearance and you won't rest until you know the ins and outs of everything. Just be careful about that curiosity though because you know what happened to the cat...!

8 TUESDAY
Moon Age Day 9   Moon Sign Aquarius

The more you look around, the greater the potential for movement and change seems to be. Not everyone wants to do what you think is best and there are at least one or two individuals who you are simply going to have to leave to their own devices. Whatever happens you need to remember that arguing won't help you now.

9 WEDNESDAY
Moon Age Day 10   Moon Sign Pisces

Forthright and challenging, you won't take anything for granted under present trends and will insist on turning over every stone in life to see what lies beneath it. This is admirable in one way but it might get you a reputation for interfering, which probably would not be helpful in the longer-term.

10 THURSDAY
Moon Age Day 11   Moon Sign Pisces

If you are involved in important meetings of any sort today it would be sensible to rehearse what you are going to say instead of shooting from the hip. The Archer is often impetuous and this certainly turns out to be the case under present astrological trends. Personalities predominate as far as your social life is concerned.

11 FRIDAY
Moon Age Day 12   Moon Sign Pisces

Today could find you to be very outspoken and slightly inclined to fly off the handle at the least provocation. Keeping your temper is the object lesson for today and this is especially true bearing in mind that some of the things that you presently believe will turn out to be simply wrong.

12 SATURDAY
Moon Age Day 13   Moon Sign Aries

Not everyone will respond in the way you wish and you need to be as flexible as possible if you want to make the most of what comes along right now. Romance is the key to the great sense of happiness that surrounds you today, and for some Sagittarians there could be overtures from surprising directions.

13 SUNDAY
Moon Age Day 14   Moon Sign Aries

This is a Sunday on which you will find it useful to talk to family members, especially those who seem to have been slightly out of sorts recently. There could be congratulations in the offing somewhere in your social circle and you need to be the first at the front of the queue to offer them.

14 MONDAY
Moon Age Day 15   Moon Sign Taurus

Although people are telling you to behave in a certain way, you have ideas of your own and these represent hunches you really should follow. Slightly quieter times could be coming along soon so make the most of the positive trends around now and go for gold. Be prepared to work even harder to achieve something you really want.

15 TUESDAY
Moon Age Day 16   Moon Sign Taurus

You may feel particularly inspired right now and it's a certainty that the unconventional side of your nature will be clearly on display. Try for a very different sort of day and take other people on the ride with you. This is not an ideal day for sticking around at home wearing your slippers.

16 WEDNESDAY
Moon Age Day 17   Moon Sign Gemini

Keep your calm and maintain an air of quiet dignity. Although this might sound easy it's far from being a normal way for Sagittarius to behave. Just remember though that people have their eyes on you and the way you behave at the moment can play an important part in what lies around the next corner.

17 THURSDAY
Moon Age Day 18   Moon Sign Gemini

Cool, calm and collected is still the best way forward, especially for the first part of today. The lunar low remains in operation, so you might have very little alternative. Co-operate with people who have good ideas but don't give away too much about your own schemes. By the end of today, the pace of life should be picking up.

18 FRIDAY
Moon Age Day 19   Moon Sign Cancer

What interests you the most today is being involved in intellectual pursuits of some sort. The more you are stimulated the better you are likely to feel and you won't be too pleased if everything is sorted out quickly and simply. You need a challenge and if one isn't forthcoming of its own accord you will find one nevertheless.

19 SATURDAY
Moon Age Day 20   Moon Sign Cancer

Personal finances are likely to be slightly less secure right now and you may need to rein in your spending a little. It isn't long until Christmas and you should look carefully at that list of potential presents before you start spoiling yourself in any way. Be aware that personality clashes are likely later in the day.

20 SUNDAY
Moon Age Day 21   Moon Sign Leo

Your persuasive powers are really good so if there is anything you really want, this is the time to go out and ask for it. Very few people could withstand a direct approach by you under present trends and you will probably get what you are looking for simply because you are so well liked.

21 MONDAY
Moon Age Day 22   Moon Sign Leo

Your main objectives and ideas are the ones that count so set too with a will and don't take no for an answer unless you know that there is no point in chasing something any further. It is definitely wise to realise when you are beaten and to simply move on in another – more fruitful – direction.

22 TUESDAY
Moon Age Day 23   Moon Sign Virgo

You have a desire for freedom but maybe not enough clear space in your life to push forward in any tangible way. Don't get bogged down with pointless details but rather be willing to look at the broad prospects for the present and future. Someone you see very rarely could be paying a return visit to your life.

23 WEDNESDAY
Moon Age Day 24   Moon Sign Virgo

If there is one thing you are striving for at the moment it is efficiency. This can be slightly frustrating if everyone else you encounter seems to be very confused and inclined to make constant mistakes. The tiring fact is that you may have to do your own job but at the same time keep an eye on colleagues.

24 THURSDAY
Moon Age Day 25   Moon Sign Libra

Life can seem fairly disheartening in a practical sense but that won't really matter because you are filled with new ideas and will be chasing these throughout most of the day. Where there are small failures, you dismiss these from your mind quickly and move on to newer and more exciting possibilities.

25 FRIDAY
Moon Age Day 26   Moon Sign Libra

If there is anything that proves to be problematic today it is likely to be emotional relationships. Although you personally remain optimistic and happy, it is likely that the same will not be true of everyone who is dear to you. It looks as though much of your time is spent supporting others.

26 SATURDAY
Moon Age Day 27   Moon Sign Libra

With a great deal of enthusiasm you plough into family life and home-based practical necessities this weekend. You are well aware that December has almost arrived and you might be putting some thought into Christmas. Be careful if you are hanging lights outside your house because you are very slightly accident-prone at present!

27 SUNDAY
Moon Age Day 28   Moon Sign Scorpio

There is a slight tendency for you to be rather outspoken today and you may be inclined to get on the wrong side of someone else as a result. The Archer is often inclined to act on impulse but present trends show how much better life would be if you learned to think ahead and to act with circumspection.

28 MONDAY
Moon Age Day 29   Moon Sign Scorpio

Your judgement is likely to be sound, which is why you know instinctively that your decisions are good and that others should follow your lead. That's fine but you will need to put your point of view across in a fairly diplomatic way because there are some very sensitive types to be dealt with.

29 TUESDAY
Moon Age Day 0   Moon Sign Sagittarius

Life now seems to be filled with potential and is likely to be far more stimulating than seems to have been the case across the last few days. Where there isn't any real incentive to do something exciting, you will find reasons yourself and you are very responsive to the needs of others right now.

30 WEDNESDAY
Moon Age Day 1   Moon Sign Sagittarius

You will start as you mean to go on today and won't have any problem at all in confronting issues that may have seemed somewhat uncomfortable only a few days ago. The middle of the working week offers the best opportunity to get ahead at work, even if social trends are confused and rather fraught.

December

2016

YOUR MONTH AT A GLANCE

$\oplus$ = Opportunities are around $\ominus$ = Be on the defensive   ● = Life is pretty ordinary

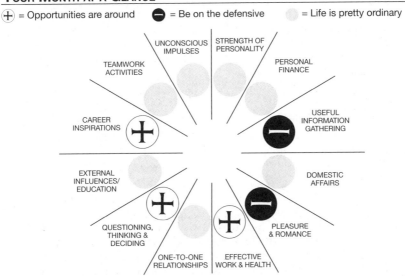

UNCONSCIOUS IMPULSES

STRENGTH OF PERSONALITY

TEAMWORK ACTIVITIES

PERSONAL FINANCE

CAREER INSPIRATIONS

USEFUL INFORMATION GATHERING

EXTERNAL INFLUENCES/ EDUCATION

DOMESTIC AFFAIRS

QUESTIONING, THINKING & DECIDING

PLEASURE & ROMANCE

ONE-TO-ONE RELATIONSHIPS

EFFECTIVE WORK & HEALTH

DECEMBER HIGHS AND LOWS

Here I show you how the rhythms of the Moon will affect you this month. Like the tide, your energies and abilities will rise and fall with its pattern. When it is above the centre line, go for it, when it is below, you should be resting.

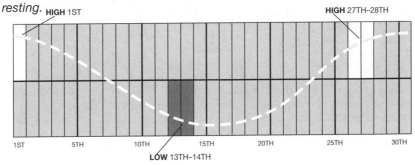

HIGH 1ST

HIGH 27TH–28TH

LOW 13TH–14TH

1ST   5TH   10TH   15TH   20TH   25TH   30TH

1 THURSDAY
Moon Age Day 2   Moon Sign Sagittarius

Once again you are firing on all cylinders and will be leading the celebrations. People love to have you around and you can enjoy every moment of what should turn out to be a red-letter day. When it comes to an emotional encounter it looks as though you have what it takes to impress and to conquer.

2 FRIDAY
Moon Age Day 3   Moon Sign Capricorn

There should be the chance today to communicate your views and ideas to someone quite important and this is a chance not to be missed. Finding the right words is rarely difficult for you and you can do yourself a great deal of good in the long-term. Attitude is all-important when it comes to romantic clinches.

3 SATURDAY
Moon Age Day 4   Moon Sign Capricorn

The Archer is in the right state of mind to indulge itself a little more than has been the case recently. You are not generally a lover of luxury and tidiness isn't your best quality but you know how you want things to be now. Avoid needless routines and tackle those tasks that you know are genuinely important.

4 SUNDAY
Moon Age Day 5   Moon Sign Aquarius

It may only now have occurred to you that Christmas is only a few weeks away and this is probably the time you should start doing something about it. You might be in the mood for some shopping though it would be too easy for you to be diverted away from possible gifts and towards something you want yourself.

5 MONDAY
Moon Age Day 6   Moon Sign Aquarius

People around you may lend you some useful assistance now if you are willing to recognise it and take it on board. Personalities abound and you won't go short of interesting company. A special someone may be about to enter your life and they could have a great bearing on your thinking in the weeks and months to come.

6 TUESDAY
Moon Age Day 7   Moon Sign Aquarius

Keep to tried-and-tested paths for the moment because some of your most innovative ideas could prove to be rather unworkable. When it comes to getting on well at work you might have to take second place to an individual you may not like very much, but an ounce of patience now may reap a ton of achievement later.

7 WEDNESDAY
Moon Age Day 8   Moon Sign Pisces

When it comes to solving problems you are second-to-none at present, even if you get rather tired of having to go through this process time and again just now. Not only are you sorting things out for yourself, you are also likely to be working hard on behalf of family members, friends and even acquaintances.

8 THURSDAY
Moon Age Day 9   Moon Sign Pisces

Talk, talk and more talk seems to be the way forward – and there's nothing especially peculiar about that for the Archer. Nevertheless there are times today when actions speak louder than words and since you can't expect everyone to follow your lead you will also have to act independently on occasion.

9 FRIDAY
Moon Age Day 10   Moon Sign Aries

Conforming to expectations is not always easy for you and could prove to be especially difficult under present trends. Don't worry about this and tell yourself that it is your originality that marks you out as being special in the eyes of those you hold most dear. A social occasion tonight could turn out to be very enjoyable.

10 SATURDAY
Moon Age Day 11   Moon Sign Aries

The search for new knowledge is never far away for the Archer and this turns out to be the case today. In most matters you know what you want and have a very good idea about how to get it. However there are moments when you will have no alternative but to rely on the help and advice of others.

11 SUNDAY
Moon Age Day 12   Moon Sign Taurus

With a few tasks having to be put on hold it could appear as though you are losing ground over your adversaries or competitors. This need not be the case and it's all down to innovative thinking on your part. Don't rush at situations but rather think them through because you will find the answers you need.

12 MONDAY
Moon Age Day 13   Moon Sign Taurus

You know best how to sort out your life and you won't be in the market for advice. Anyone who suggests they know better than you do what is right or wrong may well go away with a flea in their ear. All the same, you do need to exercise a little patience with people who are genuinely trying to help you.

13 TUESDAY
Moon Age Day 14   Moon Sign Gemini

You may have been looking forward to a warm and relaxing sort of day but with the lunar low around there are almost certainly going to be issues that are well to the forefront of your mind and which bother you. As long as you tell yourself that this is nothing more than a passing trend all should be well.

14 WEDNESDAY
Moon Age Day 15   Moon Sign Gemini

You need to realise that what you are up against today is down to nothing more than the position of the Moon, the fastest-moving of all the heavenly bodies. Any delays or uncertainties will disappear almost as quickly as they come and so the energy you put into trying to sort them out will probably be wasted.

15 THURSDAY
Moon Age Day 16   Moon Sign Cancer

You could be in for a period of significant domestic rewards and will want to make the most of the positive trends that stand around at the moment. Outside of the house you are playing things closer to your chest than might normally be the case and probably creating a deliberate air of mystery.

16 FRIDAY
Moon Age Day 17   Moon Sign Cancer

There may be some surprises today as far as your social life is concerned, and in terms of activities you have already begun the run-up to Christmas. Committing yourself exclusively to your work is going to be as difficult today as it has been so far this week and what you need most of all is variety.

17 SATURDAY
Moon Age Day 18   Moon Sign Leo

There may be additions coming along in the family, or else family members taking up with new relationships. Somewhere along the line you are going to have to open your heart to someone you didn't know before. Thank heavens you are a Sagittarian because such matters are child's play to you.

18 SUNDAY
Moon Age Day 19   Moon Sign Leo

Now is the time during December when you need to be very careful about what you are spending. The necessities of Christmas, together with a natural tendency to spread money around are a powerful and difficult combination. Before committing yourself to any purchase ask yourself if it is really necessary.

19 MONDAY
Moon Age Day 20   Moon Sign Virgo

What a good time this would be for simply talking. You will chat to loved ones and to friends and will be quite happy to put your point of view in a rational and a humorous way. Confidence tends to be fairly high at the moment and you won't be suffering too much from doubts or anxieties.

20 TUESDAY   ☿
Moon Age Day 21   Moon Sign Virgo

Pleasant social activities surround you, which is fine as long as you have the time to take part in them. There are likely to be moments today when you wish everyone would stop enjoying themselves and get down to some real work. You won't be exactly isolating yourself but you will keep up the pressure.

21 WEDNESDAY ☿
Moon Age Day 22   Moon Sign Virgo

If you want to achieve important things early in the new year, now is the time to start putting in the necessary effort. No matter how much you are committed to the festive season, in one way or another you need to look beyond it. Avoid getting tied up in red tape at any stage around now.

22 THURSDAY   ☿
Moon Age Day 23   Moon Sign Libra

You are likely to be quite restless right now and would be happy to make at least a short journey to see someone who lives at a distance. Sticking around home all the time will bore you so if you have no choice, find something useful and interesting to do. Entertaining younger family members might be a start.

23 FRIDAY   ☿
Moon Age Day 24   Moon Sign Libra

When it comes to romance you could well be entering your most positive phase for some time. This is partly because you have time to notice what is going on around you and will be less blind to the compliments coming in from a number of different directions. You have everything it takes to turn heads.

24 SATURDAY   ☿
Moon Age Day 25   Moon Sign Scorpio

You now need to get your ideas across in a big way and whilst you may be enjoying Christmas Eve in some ways, in others all the socialising does tend to get in the way. As usual you are willing to commit yourself to new plans and different strategies but others may be much less inclined to do so.

25 SUNDAY ☿ *Moon Age Day 26   Moon Sign Scorpio*

Fairly untypically for you, Christmas Day should be relaxed and marks a time when you are able to please yourself. Some Archers will have itchy feet and will be feeling the need to get out of the house. Think of someone you don't see too often and pay them a visit. You may just be very pleased that you did!

26 MONDAY ☿ *Moon Age Day 27   Moon Sign Scorpio*

Take time out to look at the details of life on Boxing Day. The branches of a tree or the patterns of raindrops on the window – these and other little things are just as important as any major issue and especially so right now. By tomorrow you will notice the pace of life increasing so a little meditation now is no bad thing.

27 TUESDAY ☿ *Moon Age Day 28   Moon Sign Sagittarius*

The lunar high arrives and it is safe to say that the Archer is really in a party mood. With the holidays in full swing you should be willing to let your hair down and to be the life and soul of any function that is going off in your vicinity. Good luck is on your side and a small, calculated gamble might be in order.

28 WEDNESDAY ☿ *Moon Age Day 29   Moon Sign Sagittarius*

You may not be working today, but if you are don't forget to set something up now that needs to be dealt with the moment the holidays are over. Your ability to concentrate is good and jobs that require that extra bit of attention are the ones you should be tackling, whether you are at work or at home.

29 THURSDAY ☿ *Moon Age Day 0   Moon Sign Capricorn*

The end of the year is approaching fast but you won't have much time today to get things sorted out for that all-important party. Maybe for once it might be good to simply join in the celebrations that are organised by others. You can still shine like the star you are and maybe even more so if you are relaxed.

30 FRIDAY ☿ *Moon Age Day 1   Moon Sign Capricorn*

Your mind is often elsewhere today and those around you who want to attract your attention might have some small problems in doing so. Personalities abound but for the moment you are slightly stuck inside your own head. Perhaps you are thinking about things you want to do in the future?

31 SATURDAY ☿   *Moon Age Day 2   Moon Sign Capricorn*

The last day of the year could easily find you happy to go with the flow and anxious to make a good impression. Fortunately you will be slightly less opinionated than might have been the case recently and far more inclined to settle for an easy life. Celebrations might start out quiet but they won't end up that way.

How to Calculate Your Rising Sign

Most astrologers agree that, next to the Sun Sign, the most important influence on any person is the Rising Sign at the time of their birth. The Rising Sign represents the astrological sign that was rising over the eastern horizon when each and every one of us came into the world. It is sometimes also called the Ascendant.

Let us suppose, for example, that you were born with the Sun in the zodiac sign of Libra. This would bestow certain characteristics on you that are likely to be shared by all other Librans. However, a Libran with Aries Rising would show a very different attitude towards life, and of course relationships, than a Libran with Pisces Rising.

For these reasons, this book shows how your zodiac Rising Sign has a bearing on all the possible positions of the Sun at birth. Simply look through the Aries table opposite.

As long as you know your approximate time of birth the graph will show you how to discover your Rising Sign.

Look across the top of the graph of your zodiac sign to find your date of birth, and down the side for your birth time (I have used Greenwich Mean Time). Where they cross is your Rising Sign. Don't forget to subtract an hour (or two) if appropriate for Summer Time.

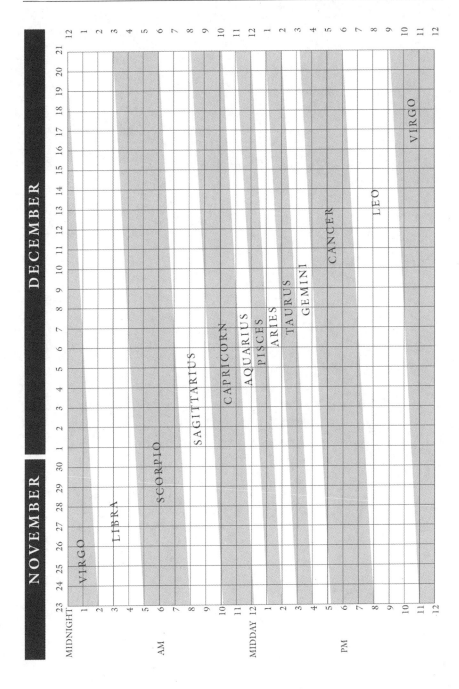

THE ZODIAC, PLANETS AND CORRESPONDENCES

The Earth revolves around the Sun once every calendar year, so when viewed from Earth the Sun appears in a different part of the sky as the year progresses. In astrology, these parts of the sky are divided into the signs of the zodiac and this means that the signs are organised in a circle. The circle begins with Aries and ends with Pisces.

Taking the zodiac sign as a starting point, astrologers then work with all the positions of planets, stars and many other factors to calculate horoscopes and birth charts and tell us what the stars have in store for us.

The table below shows the planets and Elements for each of the signs of the zodiac. Each sign belongs to one of the four Elements: Fire, Air, Earth or Water. Fire signs are creative and enthusiastic; Air signs are mentally active and thoughtful; Earth signs are constructive and practical; Water signs are emotional and have strong feelings.

It also shows the metals and gemstones associated with, or corresponding with, each sign. The correspondence is made when a metal or stone possesses properties that are held in common with a particular sign of the zodiac.

Finally, the table shows the opposite of each star sign – this is the opposite sign in the astrological circle.

Placed	Sign	Symbol	Element	Planet	Metal	Stone	Opposite
1	Aries	Ram	Fire	Mars	Iron	Bloodstone	Libra
2	Taurus	Bull	Earth	Venus	Copper	Sapphire	Scorpio
3	Gemini	Twins	Air	Mercury	Mercury	Tiger's Eye	Sagittarius
4	Cancer	Crab	Water	Moon	Silver	Pearl	Capricorn
5	Leo	Lion	Fire	Sun	Gold	Ruby	Aquarius
6	Virgo	Maiden	Earth	Mercury	Mercury	Sardonyx	Pisces
7	Libra	Scales	Air	Venus	Copper	Sapphire	Aries
8	Scorpio	Scorpion	Water	Pluto	Plutonium	Jasper	Taurus
9	Sagittarius	Archer	Fire	Jupiter	Tin	Topaz	Gemini
10	Capricorn	Goat	Earth	Saturn	Lead	Black Onyx	Cancer
11	Aquarius	Waterbearer	Air	Uranus	Uranium	Amethyst	Leo
12	Pisces	Fishes	Water	Neptune	Tin	Moonstone	Virgo